Beethoven as Physicist

EIR Contents

www.larouchepub.com Volume 44, Number 52, December 29, 2017

*Cover
This Week*

*Ludwig van
Beethoven*

BEETHOVEN AS PHYSICIST

I. Strategic Report

3 ZEPP-LAROUCHE WEBCAST
Time To End the Reign of Geopolitics

11 BITCOIN: A PERSPECTIVE FROM FRANCE
The Ultimate Madness of the Trans-Atlantic Speculative Bubble
by Stephanie Ezrol

14 MUELLER'S FRAUD EXPOSED
Neocons Escalate Push for Geopolitical Confrontation
by Harley Schlanger

19 Houston's Mayor Leads Trade Mission to China
by Brian Lantz

II. Our Cultural-Political Offensive

22 CHRISTMAS CONCERT, DEC. 16
Beethoven at Co-Cathedral of St. Joseph
by Lynn Yen

23 DEC. 16 SCHILLER INSTITUTE CONCERT PROGRAM NOTES
Beethoven's 'New Song,' The Mass in C Major, Op. 86
by Dennis Speed

26 SCHILLER INSTITUTE NYC CHORUS
Christmas Concert on Beethoven's Birthday in Brooklyn
by Diane Sare

28 Detroit and LaRouche's Fourth Law
by Susan Kokinda

III. Lyndon LaRouche's Original Work

31 Beethoven as a Physical Scientist
by Lyndon H. LaRouche, Jr.
November 2, 1988

ZEPP-LAROUCHE WEBCAST

Time To End the Reign of Geopolitics

This is an edited transcript of the Dec. 21 weekly webcast of the founder of the Schiller Institutes, Helga Zepp-LaRouche. A video of the webcast can be found at *newparadigm.schillerinstitute.com.*

Harley Schlanger: Hello, I'm Harley Schlanger from the Schiller Institute. Welcome to this week's Schiller Institute International Webcast, featuring Helga Zepp-LaRouche, founder of the Schiller Institutes and also the president of the German Schiller Institute.

We have been in the forefront of the very significant developments that took place this week. We will discuss them today to get our audience abreast of these issues and strategic developments, including the continuing evidence of the corrupt and immoral practices of the Special Counsel Robert Mueller. There are now Congressmen calling for shutting down the investigation and even putting some of these people in jail. This is occurring just as we are expanding our distribution of the Mueller dossier.

It's also a moment of very grave danger. There's a good reason why wars and terrorist events, and false flag attacks often occur at the end of the Summer and during the Christmas season—mainly because people aren't paying attention. So we have to make sure that people *are* paying attention as we enter this crucial period at the end of 2017.

Now, I'd like to begin with the national security strategic doctrine that was just released by the President and the administration. Helga, you've pointed to the differences between what Trump said and the language of the doctrine. There are some differences, but one of the key problems, as you identified, is that this is part of the "old geopolitics." So I'd like you to discuss what you mean by that and why that's a significant problem.

Helga Zepp-LaRouche: The paper was written by a woman named Dr. Nadia Schadlow, who is said to be close to H.R. McMaster, and worked earlier in the vicinity of Bush and Cheney. She comes from an army background. This document looks at the world from the standpoint of, as you said, geopolitics,—and if you look at it from that standpoint, then of course China and Russia, but especially China which is rising, are regarded as rivals or enemies. Trump, in a very unusual move, insisted that he present the paper, rather than the National Security Advisor who normally presents such a report. It seems that he did that in order to soften certain formulations. For example: Apart from going through some of the language of the report, he also said that he wants to build a very strong partnership with Russia and China. This had the

President Donald Trump with his National Security Advisor, H.R. McMaster.

ridiculous effect with some European newspapers commenting, "he can't even read the paper," because he said things which are different than the report. It reflects the fact that the faction fight in the Trump administration is far from being over—that there is still an effort by the neocons and by leftovers of previous administrations, in various parts of this administration, which expressed themselves in this report. And Trump, who after all had a very successful state visit to China a little while ago and who has talked successfully on the telephone with Putin in the last week, defeating a terrorist attack that was planned for St. Petersburg. Trump still has the inclination that he wants to work with Russia and China.

But I think if you look at the extremely sharp reactions coming from the Russian Foreign Ministry, from Dmitry Peskov, the spokesman of the Kremlin, from China's *Global Times* newspaper, from the Chinese Foreign Ministry, and from the Chinese Embassy in Washington—they all say that this doctrine reflects an outmoded kind of thinking. They point to the fact that there is a completely new era shaping especially the West Pacific—one of the six regions discussed in this paper. This is one of the areas which has been changed completely through the Belt and Road Initiative, where all the countries in the region are cooperating with China in "win-win" cooperation to the mutual benefit of each of them. And therefore, since the offer has been made many times to the United States, and to Europe, to cooperate with the Belt and Road Initiative, there is actually no reason to go into such an adversarial position. The Russians called it an "imperial document," and insist that it still reflects the desire to insist on a unipolar world, which is long gone, so it's a completely futile effort. And the Chinese were also extremely critical, saying that this is an "outmoded way of thinking" and cannot lead to anything positive.

It shows you that the world is still very far from being out of the danger zones. I normally give credit to Trump, because unlike his predecessors Bush and Obama, he has extended his hand to Russia and China, and he still has the potential to move the world in a different direction. Nevertheless, when he does something which I'm not so happy about, I take the liberty to say so.

It is interesting that of all places, the *Wall Street Journal* had an article yesterday, "The New Era of Global Stability," by Arthur Herman, who is still thinking in geopolitical terms. He says that given the fact that you have three men—Trump, Xi Jinping, and Putin—who are all working in what he calls "a balance of power,"—which I don't think is the right expression—but he says, therefore we have left behind the Wilsonian age of permanent wars which led the world to almost continuous wars, in Korea, in Vietnam, in Afghanistan, in Libya, Syria, and so forth. He says that age is now over because of these three men.

I think there is a completely different quality to that relationship, and the potential of that relationship—namely, what Xi Jinping calls a "community for a shared future of mankind." What we normally call humanity united for the "common aims of mankind"—*that* is the potential.

We are in one of these areas, and one of the commentaries in one Chinese paper said that there are many different conceptions about how the future of mankind should be shaped, and that it is not yet a settled question. And I think that that is absolutely true, but that is why it is so absolutely important to overcome the geopolitical view which insists that groups of countries, or one country, have a legitimate interest against the others. That is the kind of thinking which led to two world wars in the Twentieth Century, and I think it should be obvious to anybody that in the age of thermonuclear weapons, that thinking can only lead to the possible annihilation of the human species: We should get rid of it.

Schlanger: I've received several emails from viewers who have said they agree with a lot of what we say, but they don't understand why you're so focussed on this question of geopolitics, because they say, "isn't geopolitics the natural order?" in international relations. You've basically answered that question, but is there anything else you'd like to say on that? Because I think this is the crucial issue, coming up as it does around this national strategic document.

Zepp-LaRouche: The only way to look at it is from the long arc of the evolution of the human species. In the beginning, when you still had tribal formations and little ethnic groupings, people had various ways of settling conflict—either diplomacy or negotiations—and if that didn't work, conflict and war. That was a characteristic of human development for a very long time. I don't think that is the true nature of mankind, because if you continue with the idea that if all negotiations and diplomacy fail, you still can resort to war—in the age of thermonuclear weapons this would be the end of civilization. This idea of using war as a means of conflict resolution, corresponds to the age of maybe four-year-old little boys who think it's all right to kick each other in the knee. I think humanity has the potential of becoming adult, that you can, indeed—through negotiation, and especially through the establishment of a higher order of collaboration in the interest of everybody—that you can establish a way of the human governance worldwide, where war is no longer a method of resolving conflict.

Much of this way of thinking comes from the great thinker of the Fifteenth Century, Nicholas of Cusa, who is the father of modern science, and who is also the father of the idea of the sovereign nation-state. He developed a method of thinking which he called the *coincidentia oppositorum*, the coincidence of opposites. He said that because man is capable of creative reason, that you can think on a higher order where conflicts on a lower order disappear. This is the argument that the One has a higher power than the Many. That thinking went into the Peace of Westphalia—the idea that you can overcome conflict by establishing a common interest. And even if perhaps Nicholas of Cusa is not very well known in China, yet still I think that probably because of the Confucian tradition, the idea of the New Silk Road, the Belt and Road Initiative of Xi Jinping, reflects exactly that philosophical approach.

So, if mankind were to become adult, we would not waste any more energy on stupid things like chasing money, stock market speculation, and other things which are really a waste of time. People would become creative and relate to the creativity of the other, and that not only between people, but also among nations. So I think that that is the right way to look at things, and not from the standpoint of eternal Aristotelian conflict between A and B, one geopolitical group against another. Instead, the Cusan view of the coincidence of opposites, the one humanity first, is the better way to look at it.

Schlanger: I had some experience recently resolving conflict between three and four year-olds, and I can assure you that adult supervision is absolutely necessary, and that's what you've been talking about in terms of the Cusan approach.

We saw something completely crazy in the last days, from *Newsweek* magazine and *Bildzeitung*, again,

Missile units carrying out the first electronic launch by the Russian Iskander short range tactical ballistic missile system, seen here July 12, 2017, in Zabaykalsky Krai, Russia. The missile is designed for use by Russian ground forces.

bringing up the specter of the Russian army overrunning Europe. What's wrong with these people?

Christmas Surprise for Bob Mueller?

Zepp-LaRouche: Well, it is very clear that the Russian maneuvers, Zapad 2017, which the *Newsweek* article and also the *Bildzeitung* referred to, was a demonstration on the side of Russia that they intend to defend their country. It is a reaction to the whole NATO policy of encirclement, of moving more and more troops to the Russian border. But the idea that Russia would move to occupy the three Baltic states, bomb Poland with Iskander missiles from Kaliningrad, and bomb infrastructure of Germany, Sweden and Finland—that's just completely absurd! This would never happen.

It's just a scare story, among other things to create a motivation for a conventional buildup. These articles also come in the context of the decision of the European Council to create a European defense union, which is a completely ridiculous idea. This will not make the EU more integrated. On the contrary, it will only cause more opposition.

It's an expression of those people who absolutely oppose the new paradigm, who want to use geopolitics—it's the old British manipulation, "divide and conquer," play the weaker against the stronger and vice

CSPAN

Congressman Devin Nunes (R-Calif.), Chairman of the House Intelligence Committee, is investigating the FBI. Shown here on Dec. 19, 2017.

CSPAN

Rep. Trey Gowdy at a Dec. 7, 2013 House Judiciary Committee hearing which questioned FBI Director Christopher Wray.

FBI

Robert Mueller

versa, and in that way keep control. So it's really a tool of the oligarchists and imperialists to keep to the old order, but I don't think it has any chance of success.

Schlanger: Speaking of the old order, we've seen the continuation of the Mueller investigation. But we now are seeing something different emerge: There were the scandals around Andrew McCabe, the deputy director of the FBI; Strzok and his mistress writing text messages to each other about the necessity to prevent Trump from becoming President, or to have an "insurance policy" were he to become President. There's also Bruce Ohr and his wife who are part of the Fusion GPS crowd.

Now, this led to comments from Rep. Trey Gowdy (R-SC), the Chairman of the House Oversight and Government Reform Committee, who said these scandals demonstrate "unprecedented bias." Jim Jordan, the Republican Congressman from Ohio, said "Everything points to the fact that there was an orchestrated plan to try to prevent Donald Trump from becoming the President of the United States." Senate Judiciary chair Chuck Grassley is calling for firing some of these people. What is it going to take to shut down the Mueller investigation, given all these exposes coming out right now?

Zepp-LaRouche: There are rumors circulating that Trump may come out with a "Christmas surprise." If that were to happen, it would be an interesting thing. It could be the appointment of somebody to investigate this whole complex, in the form of a special investigator. But I think also, already now, these congressmen and senators you mentioned, Nunes, Grassley in the Senate, Gowdy, and Gaetz, and various others—I think they're quite fired up already about what they're finding.

Even the European media are not entirely covering it up any more. There was a quite good article in Denmark, in the conservative daily *Berlingske Tidende*, which said that Obama bureaucrats conspired to prevent the election of Trump, and after that failed they're trying to topple him; and then they go through the whole story of who the culprits are. So it is coming out. Even the major German daily *FAZ* could not avoid reporting it, even though, in their typical way, they tried to downplay it and say, all these people who say there is a "Deep State," are conspiracy theorists, and so on. But the truth is coming out.

We in the United States, that is, our colleagues from LaRouche PAC, have launched a full mobilization with many activists; they distributed the dossier about Mueller to all the Congressional offices. They had many in-depth discussions, amidst increasing interest. It seems that some people in the Congress realize that what's at stake is the Constitution of the United States. Congress has oversight rights over the intelligence agencies, and if these agencies are loyal to a previous administration which was involved in such incredible schemes, they are aware of the fact that if they don't act right now, then you can throw the Constitution of the United States in the wastepaper basket.

But I think it will require a continuous effort and mobilization, because the people on the other side are quite desperate. They see that their whole system is coming down. Several people said that what was done by the Department of Justice, or some people in it and in the FBI, were felonies. They are trying to twist the situation to avoid the consequences of their acts. It's reaching a very, very serious point, the tide is already turning. But it is a fight, so stay tuned with us, and don't be complacent. Don't eat too many cookies over Christmas: Stay tuned and stay mobilized.

Schlanger: And I also think it's important that we provide a certain kind of leadership that's essential, which is to identify not just the connectos and the names and the corruption, but the *intent*. This again gets to the thing you were talking about in the beginning, the attempt to stop President Trump from having a strategic-cooperation alliance with Russia and China. James Clapper, the former Director of National Intelligence, stuck his foot in his mouth once again, saying, "Putin knows how to handle an asset, and that's what he's doing with the President."

So I think it's crucial that we get people to understand that this is not just about Trump's character, or people not liking Trump, but it has to do with the whole shift into a new paradigm, as we've been discussing.

Now, on that, you talked a little bit before about the situation in Europe. There's a whole series of crises brewing, in East Europe, and the banking situation. There's been a statement from a prominent Italian economist that the euro is "fascist." What's going on? What's the latest on the situation in Europe?

Zepp-LaRouche: This Italian economist is very critical of the euro, for similar reasons to why we have been critical, or for example, the late Professor Hankel who had laid out the argument quite well, that the Euro-

Martin Schultz, when he was President of the European Parliament.

zone was never an optimal currency zone, because some countries which had a rural character, and you had industrialized countries. And further, Europe is not a country, there is no European people. It's not like the United States, and it's not even like Latin America; because you have almost 30 nations, cultures, traditions. People in one country, in Slovenia for example, know absolutely nothing about people in Alsace-Lorraine. There is just no way that you can even know, because you can't read their newspapers—even if the newspapers don't report much anyway. So there is no European people.

And what this Italian Professor Bagnai said is that even if the supporters of the euro don't wear "black shirts," nevertheless, anybody who plans to implement his goal through violence represents a form of fascism. And what he's referring to is that everybody knows the euro does not function; he said it's written in all the textbooks, that it's only a question of time until this euro construction collapses; and then, that crisis is intended to lead to a further, forced European integration—and he says, that is fascism.

Now, that is not as far-fetched as some people may think. Because for example, Jacques Attali, who was the key advisor and *eminence grise* of France in the time of Mitterrand, had said many times that the fathers of the euro deliberately created it with a "birth defect," so that it would come to a crisis, and then that crisis would be used to implement the political union which could not be put through otherwise. That is, there is very clearly a *big* opposition against the idea of a "United States of Europe," for the reason that I said earlier—that there is no European people.

So there are these calls right now: French President Macron, European Council President Juncker, German social-democratic leader Martin Schulz, they all have given only slightly different versions of an idea that, now, because of all of these crises—the refugees, the tensions among the different East and West European countries—that one should impose a "United States of Europe." I think this has as much chance as a snowflake in hell, because all these efforts to impose a supranational construct which eliminates even more sovereignty, will only cause more opposition and more reaction. So I think it will not work.

I find it quite significant that several advisors of Hungarian Prime Minister Orban have said that this discussion about a "United States of Europe" reminds them of Hitler. So the tone has become quite sharp, and I think it's very far from unity.

And the latest atrocity, so to speak, is the fact that the European Union has decided to apply Article 7 to Poland, taking its voting rights away. Now, first of all, this will also not work, because this could only be implemented if there were unity among the other 26 states, but Hungary already said they will not back the decision of the EU against Poland—and they're now talking about similar measures against Romania. I think all of this will just lead to more controversy, and more disunity, and if they keep doing this, Poland may even leave the EU, because under no circumstances will they back down.

Schlanger: And just quickly, on the crisis in Europe, anything on the non-government situation in Germany?

Zepp-LaRouche: Oh, that is a terrible situation, because, you know it's now almost three months since the election, and first, the so-called "Jamaica" [black, gold, green] coalition talks failed. Now, they're talking about a Grand Coalition between the Christian Democrats and the Social-Democrats of the SPD. Merkel says only that she will only accept a coalition as the outcome, while the SPD says, no, they want to have an open-ended discussion, maybe resulting in support for a minority government—which Merkel has ruled out. All of this is going on and on and on, and I think the biggest problem with this is that none of the participating parties has any vision of what the future of Germany should be—where should Europe be in 10 or 100 years from now? So it's all about power politics; it's about position; it's about little issues, and it just means there's no government in sight before Easter, they're now saying.

But naturally, no decision will be made for Europe until you have a German government, so the whole situation in Europe is extremely fragile right now. And you know, many more countries are taking that as a reason to ally more and more with the Silk Road. Austria, Switzerland, the East Europeans, the Balkan countries, Italy, Spain, and Portugal—they are all strengthening their ties with the Belt and Road Initiative, and that is a very good thing. And it means the position of resistance maintained by Brussels and Berlin will not be tenable for very long.

A Meltdown of the System

Schlanger: From the United States, this last couple of days, there was the passage of so-called tax reform bill. I know you have some thoughts on this. This is not going to solve any problems: What do you have to say about it, Helga?

Zepp-LaRouche: This is celebrated as the first big victory of President Trump. I don't think it will solve anything, if you don't put it in a package of other measures, including Glass-Steagall, and a credit system like Roosevelt's Reconstruction Finance Corporation or the National Bank of Alexander Hamilton, and end the speculation in the derivatives sector. If you only lower taxes under these circumstances, without curbing the other factors I just mentioned, what it probably will do, is it will attract some investment in the United States for sure, but people in Germany are already saying, "well, we have to protect ourselves, and take countermeasures against it," so it will lead to an increased tension internationally. Probably in the United States, today's big corporations and banks will just use these tax cuts to invest more in the stock market, in buying up their own shares, which they have been doing since the crisis of 2008 with Quantitative Easing and the zero-interest-rate policy. One reason why this is to be feared, is that Jamie Dimon, for example, laughed, and said: This is wonderful, this is Quantitative Easing 4.

A bitcoin token.

I think it just requires a continuation of our mobilization. I know our colleagues in the United States from LaRouche PAC have produced a new pamphlet with the demand implementing the Four Laws of my husband, Lyndon LaRouche, and showing why the United States must join with China in building the New Silk Road, both domestically and internationally. This pamphlet, "LaRouche's Four Laws & America's Future on the New Silk Road," is out. I would encourage you, our viewers and listeners, to get hold of this document: Read it, because it has all the solutions—the correct economic conceptions for the United States and the rest of the world to get out of this present crisis.

This is all extremely urgent, because we could have a meltdown of the system any minute.

Let me mention briefly, this bitcoin mania which is going on, is really a reminder of the Dutch Tulip Bubble in 1637 before it burst. China has recognized that danger, they're banning speculation in bitcoins. And all of these mad crazes just make clear, the urgent need to implement Glass-Steagall, and the entire Four Laws of Mr. LaRouche, which include a massive increase in the productivity of the workforce through a crash program in fusion technology, in space cooperation, and in high-tech investments in general, including high-technology infrastructure.

The recent Amtrak accident in Washington State just underlines that this is absolutely necessary. Unless this is all done as a package, I don't think the world will get out of this crisis.

Schlanger: Helga, I'd like to conclude with a question that again has come up from several viewers: People fall prey to this idea that somehow China is a threat, and one of the things that people have picked up on is this concept of "Socialism with Chinese characteristics." Now, you've written extensively on this, and it's not fair to ask you to summarize it in a couple of minutes, but that's what I'm going to do!

What does Xi Jinping mean by "Socialism with Chinese characteristics"?

Zepp-LaRouche: I think you also find right now, a growing self-confidence among the Chinese, who point to the fact that nobody can debate the incredible success of the Chinese model of economy. And they point to the fact that their model is clearly very, very much superior and more successful than the Western model, which they refuse to follow.

Now, there is such a thing as the determinative value of facts. And people should ask themselves, why is the Chinese model more successful? Well, the answer is very simple—that it is primarily devoted to the common good. This is always criticized by the West, with claims that China is suppressing freedom and human rights, and so forth. But in reality, if you ask yourself, is this complete mega-individualistic hedonism of the West— is that really a value which is so desirable? Values which have reached a point, where *everything goes*, everything is allowed. There are no more criteria for truth, or for the acceptance of the common good, everything is the survival of the fittest, and those who are rich become richer, and those who have the misfortune to be poor become poorer—is that really so desirable?

In China, I'm convinced that while there is debate about Marx, and there is a debate about socialism with Chinese characteristics, yet I'm absolutely convinced— and I have looked at it for a long time and from many aspects—that what is meant by "Chinese characteristics," refers to the two and half thousand years of Confucian tradition in China. I have written an article at the beginning of this year, actually, pointing to the affinity of the ideas of the German poet Friedrich Schiller and Confucius, who both have an image of man, that man has the moral obligation to self-perfect his entire life or her entire life, in order to serve the common good better and more efficiently.

Obviously, sometimes that means that individual rights are curtailed a little bit for the common good. One very good example was the building of the Three Gorges Dam, where people in the West were completely hysterical and said, "oh, these poor peasants, who have to be moved so this dam could be built, this is trampling on freedom and human rights." Well, but what if you take the view that with this dam you had an enormous gain of hydropower, and that thousands and thousands of people would not drown every time the river flooded? Maybe it is better to act in the common good, and indeed these very peasants got other living quarters that were much more modern and much better. So this is a typical example of what can be done if you put the common good first. That is what China has very clearly done, and they have lifted more than 700 million people out of poverty. They also have a very clear plan to move the remaining 42 million poor people out of poverty by 2020, and they're acting very effectively to do that. We may have mentioned that already, but I'll say it again: They locate where the poor people are, which regions they live in, and then they ask what are the reasons for the poverty— what has to be done to address it, to get them out of it? They use e-commerce, for instance, to allow the farmers in far distant rural areas to market their products. They're moving very, very efficiently to uplift the entire population out of poverty.

Now, how many poor people are there in the United States, how many homeless? We heard figures in the last period, the unbelievable figure that 10% of all schoolchildren in New York come from homeless backgrounds. That doesn't mean they live on the streets, but they don't have their own home. In Europe there are 90 million poor, and nobody is talking about lifting them out of poverty. The rate of poverty in Greece, just increased, whereby I think two-thirds of the whole population is below the poverty line and have incomes of below 1,000 euros; and a very high percentage of that, again, have only part-time jobs, earning something like 450 euros per month. And there is no plan to change that—on the contrary, the EU is implementing more vicious austerity all the time.

I think that people should not look at this China question with prejudice. The Chinese model is completely different: It's based on 2,500 years of tradition, and there is something to this Chinese way of approaching things through peaceful approaches, through a "win-win" offer which is really a better model of governance. And people shouldn't be so prejudiced. I have found that most people know nothing about China. You have a few, a handful of people who have been there, who do business

A homeless person sleeping on a bench in Greece.

there, and they are completely excited about the options which the New Silk Road is offering to the world. They are *really* transformed and totally excited.

Because of the negative media, there are many people who still believe in the Chinese threat, who believe in the "yellow peril," and other decades-old propaganda campaigns. I think it's a shame: Because if you look at China without prejudice, it is an incredibly interesting culture—it's rich, it's 5,000 old, it has produced beautiful things in music, in poetry, and in philosophy. It's already one of the vanguard countries in science—it's an innovative country. So I would suggest that people, rather than simply believing what I'm saying—start to investigate China and look for yourself. And you will find that it is completely different from what the Western media or some of the geopolitical think-tanks are trying to tell you. And you will discover beautiful things, I promise.

Schlanger: On that uplifting note, Helga, on behalf of the Schiller Institute, I'd like to wish people a Merry Christmas, but with your suggestion: Don't just eat cookies and drink rum punch. Use your holiday as an opportunity to reflect on the great opportunities for mankind today, and what it means to have the Christmas Spirit, and in that sense the Christmas Spirit and the Silk Road Spirit should be one and the same.

So Helga, we'll see you next week! Thanks a lot.

Zepp-LaRouche: Yes, Merry Christmas.

The Ultimate Madness of the Trans-Atlantic Speculative Bubble

by Stephanie Ezrol

The following report is adapted from an article posted Dec. 21, 2017 on the French-language website Solidarité et Progrès, *and from other Europe-based discussions which included former French presidential candidate Jacques Cheminade,* EIR *founder Lyndon H. LaRouche, Jr., and Schiller Institute President Helga Zepp-LaRouche, on the subject of the Bitcoin bubble.*

Dec. 25—The story has often been told that in 1929 a rich bootlegger, Joseph Kennedy (father of the future president of the United States) was having his shoes shined by his usual shoeshine guy. At one point, the guy looked up at him and said, "Mr. Kennedy, I've got a super stock tip for you."

Kennedy listened, but immediately concluded that if shoe-shine men were now speculating on the market, it was time to sell everything. In fact, the market had topped out: Kennedy sold his shares just before the crash, and became one of the richest men in America in the 1930s.

Today, the bitcoin mania is spreading in regions hard-hit by the economic crisis, causing a dopamine-serotonin infused mental frenzy, attracting "investors" ranging from ill-informed little old ladies to retirees in Darien, Connecticut.

It's only the most extreme aspect of the whole Ponzi scheme of the financial and monetarist system of the West that goes back to the 1971 break-up of FDR's Bretton Woods agreements, which break-up was a result of America's post-FDR collaboration with the British empire speculators and financial predators initiated by President Truman—a collaboration Lyndon LaRouche had warned would lead to unprecedented disaster.

This bubble is proof for people who still are willing to think, of how this system is becoming absolutely insane. The new paradigm, for which Helga Zepp-LaRouche has become a major international spokesperson and leader, is something more than just the new railroads and other impressive infrastructure of China's New Silk Road. It's a new spirit: it means that you don't take money or power from the other, but you create a win-win system, a new order, to produce, and to develop and increase your knowledge of the universe and the beauty of your life with the other.

Crime, Delirium, and Greed

The spectacular surge of "cryptocurrency" is causing consternation throughout the financial press and the media. We have had many private discussions with people who are warning against the "mainstreaming" of bitcoin derivatives, even with people who are not what you would call moral in their economic perspective; they are not concerned about the well-being of people, about human values. But they're afraid. They are "market conservatives." But they're afraid, scared of their own Frankenstein monster. It's something which is becoming bigger and bigger.

One bitcoin was worth only a few cents at their creation in 2009. Its price was $4,000 last

Dramatic speculative increase of the bitcoin price.

August, and reached nearly $20,000 in mid-December. While China, Morocco, and South Korea have put measures in place to ban them, Japan has legalized them, and the international financial institutions are promoting them. On December 7, there were reports in Reuters and Bloomberg that Goldman Sachs "is planning to clear bitcoin futures for some clients as the new contracts go live on exchanges." On December 10, the CME Group inaugurated the first futures market for bitcoin on its CME and CBOT (Chicago Mercantile Exchange and Chicago Board of Trade) exchanges. It is reported that the Nasdaq Stock Exchange is planning to start trading bitcoin futures during the first half of 2018.

We live today, in many ways, in George Orwell's dystopia (or is it Bertrand Russell's utopia?), where we manage to make believe that black is white, or that injustice is just. In the same way we have been made to believe that bitcoins (and other cryptocurrencies) are an alternative to "the system," although they are nothing but one of its most extreme and perverse expressions. It is entirely consistent with the libertarian project inspired by one of the designers of modern ultra-liberalism, Friedrich von Hayek, promoter of "private" currencies independent of any state. Heralding cryptocurrencies as an alternative, is to pass control to a system in which currencies have been effec-

tively removed from state control, where control is then in the hands of central bank and private bank "counterfeiters." This mania truly marks the end of the road!

Bitcoin is not based on anything real. A team of Australian researchers from the University of Technology Sydney and Sydney University, has just completed a study, "Sex, Drugs and Bitcoin," showing that nearly half of all bitcoin transactions are associated with the purchase or sale of illegal goods and services, including drugs, stolen weapons and pirated software. The vast majority of "legal" users are like Joseph Kennedy's shoe-shine man, buying and holding bitcoin, waiting for its price to rise.

In mid-December, French associates of the LaRouche movement went to the "Maison du Bitcoin," at 35 Rue du Caire in the Paris financial district. They reported that the fever of greed in the average person, created by "magic money," was quite palpable, speaking to several people in the vicinity. One person said, "It's all about retiring at the right time." Another informed us, "Bitcoin—that's a has-been. Invest in Ripple!" A third explained, "I'm here to get information. My employer's wealth manager—she herself is an elderly woman—sent me here to get information." A thirty-something fellow, who had invested in bitcoin when it was worth only a few cents,

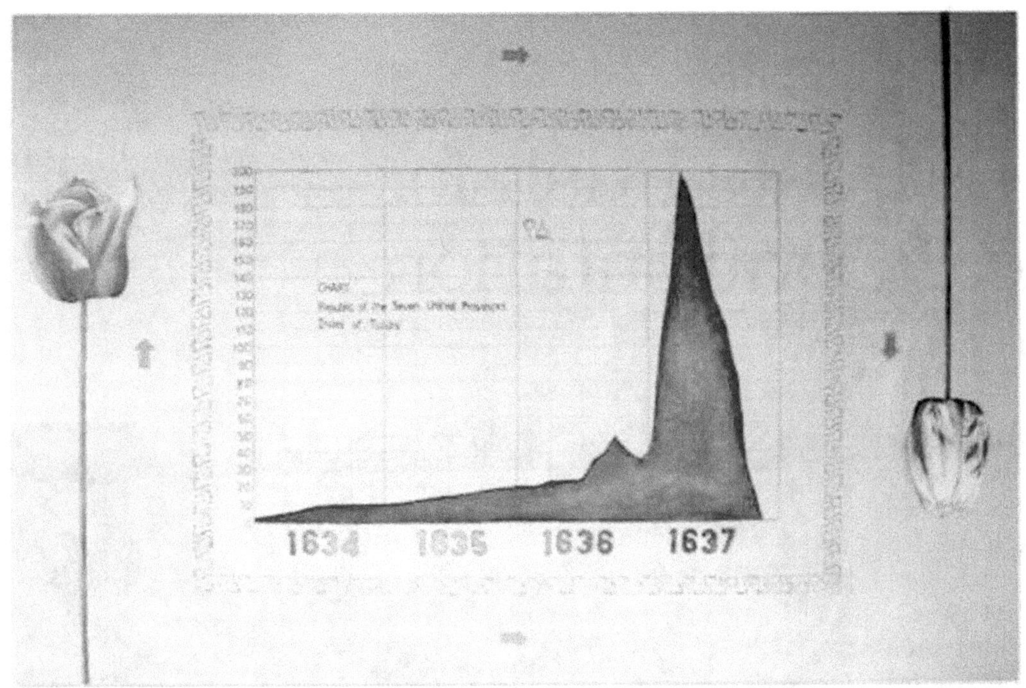

Graph of the speculative 1637 Tulip Bubble rise and crash.

was cashing everything out that day, and becoming a millionaire. To our question, "Are you greedy?" He replied, "Of course I am. Insiders like me get to make the big bucks because there are gullible fools now buying in!"

Will this be the detonator to crash the Trans-Atlantic system?

Financial analysts are now comparing the bitcoin price spike with the 1637 Dutch tulip bubble that triggered a crisis of the entire system. As Ambrose Evans-Pritchard wrote in the *Daily Telegraph* on Dec. 14, "The 'everything bubble' is about to burst."

There is a 21 million limit to the issuance of bitcoins, and the closer we approach this fateful figure, the scarcer the tradeable currency becomes, driving the soaring price. Bitcoin value in dollars has increased by more than 1,700% since the beginning of the year. The total mass today represents about $400 billion.

Economist Daniel Cohen analyzes the phenomenon, in his Dec. 9 opinion column, "What the Bitcoin Madness Reveals," in the French newspaper *L'Obs*: "In a world looking for the dream of maximum return, bitcoin has indeed become the fantasy machine. In one year, its price had multiplied tenfold, in two years by a hundred!" Cohen continues, "Everything has been done to create a resemblance to gold. You can 'dig' bitcoin mines, like gold miners, by solving complex algorithms that earn free bitcoins," but "bitcoin still is, despite the verbiage, nothing but a financial bubble. The buyers hold it not for its intrinsic value—it has none—but to sell it at a higher price to the next sucker. When there are no more to be found, the bubble will burst."

Bitcoin benefits tax evaders, says Daniel Cohen. "It offers all the Mafiosi of the world an ideal means of payment: secure, immaterial, and outside the public sphere. However, this madness can only flourish because public authorities allow it. The day they decide to ban it, waking up to the fact that it derives its value from its link to illegality, bitcoin will be immediately demonetized."

The problem is that a lot of people in Europe—most people in Europe—can't believe that the sky can ever become blue again. They are in a sort of gray or black zone. Lyndon LaRouche's French associates report that they are committed to really giving them the sense that they have a power to change things: that's what has happened with China, it's happening, in a sense, with Russia, and with Trump. Then, you create in people's minds a new understanding of the situation, because they will be able to see it from above. We have a lot of good reactions in broader circles to that totally realistic strategic optimism.

Lyndon LaRouche, a participant in this European-based discussion, happily concluded "we could probably do the job very nicely, if we just did the job right." With people in various parts of the planet, we can be the catalyst to do what is needed to be done, simply by talking to people carefully about what has to be done. Human beings have the power; we have the power to build a force, a greater force than has existed before—and we can win.

Neocons Escalate Push for Geopolitical Confrontation

by Harley Schlanger

Dec. 22—The urgency of defeating the efforts of special counsel Robert Mueller to conduct a coup against elected U.S. President Trump, on behalf of British and Wall Street imperial interests, can be seen in the attempt by neocons both within the administration and outside, to insist that the U.S. must continue the policy of geopolitical confrontation with Russia and China, which was supported by his opponents. In the last days, there are further indications that it is Trump's continuing commitment to strategic collaboration with Russia and China that precipitated "Russiagate"—not so-called meddling in the U.S. election by Russian President Putin, nor "collusion" by Trump with Putin to steal the election, that has made him a target of unprecedented vitriolic attacks, lying media stories, and a corrupt "investigation" which his opponents hope will lead to his ouster.

Xinhua/Yin Bogu

U.S. National Security Advisor H.R. McMaster.

Throughout the 2016 campaign, Trump aggressively targeted both the Bush Republicans and the Obama-Hillary Clinton Democrats as supporters of endless wars, which have resulted in millions of casualties and wasted of trillions of dollars, while America has become less safe. He launched devastating attacks against the Bush Administration, accusing President George W. Bush of "lying" to get the U.S. into a war with Iraq, and against Obama and Clinton, for the policy of "regime change" in Libya, and the attempt to oust Syrian President Assad at the risk of a war with Russia. He also blasted the deployment of U.S. and NATO troops eastward, targeting Russia, saying he was convinced that it would be "great" if the U.S. and Russia would be friends and allies, especially in the war against terrorists. He said at several campaign events that he would have no neocons in his administration.

The war-weary American people responded to his attacks on the neocon wars, by electing him President. The neocons responded to his election by launching Russiagate!

The release this week of a National Security Strategy document reveals that neocons within Trump's administration are trying to steer the administration into confrontation with both Russia and China. The document portrays both nations as pursuing policies directly counter to U.S. interests. In the introduction, the document claims that "China and Russia challenge American power, influence and interests, attempting to erode American security and prosperity. They are determined to make economies less free and less fair, to grow their militaries, and to control information and data to repress their societies and expand their influence."

Later, the document asserts that Russia and China "want to shape a world antithetical to U.S. values and interests." In a passage which is a thinly-veiled attack on the Belt-and-Road Initiative, China is singled out as seeking "to displace the United States in the Indo-Pacific Region, expand the reaches of its state-driven economic model, and reorder the region in its favor," while Russia is accused of seeking "to restore its great power status and establish spheres of influence near its borders." President Xi's "win-win" approach, embodied in his New Silk Road policy, which would replace geopolitical confrontation with pursuit of common goals, is falsely characterized as a plan by China to dominate its neighbors economically, with military threats to back it up.

In commenting on the document, Trump's National Security Advisor General H.R. McMaster explicitly endorsed geopolitics in a speech delivered to the U.K.-based think-tank Policy Exchange, stating "Geopolitics are back with a vengeance, after this holiday from history we took in the so-called post-Cold War period." He identified both Russia and China as strategic adversaries. It is reported that the document reflects the views of McMaster and two assistants who participated in drafting it, Nadia Schadlow, a deputy assistant for National Strategic Strategy, and Dina Powell, deputy National Security Adviser and a Goldman Sachs alumnus. Both Schadlow and Powell served in the administration of George W. Bush.

Schiller Institute President Helga Zepp-LaRouche has called this language an attempt to return the United States to the "neocon geopolitical confrontation" approach of the two previous administrations, pointing to sharp denunciations by Russian and Chinese officials, who denounced the document as an example of "old, outdated thinking." But Mrs. LaRouche also pointed out that President Trump himself, in releasing the document, was less confrontational, as he said he will "attempt to build a great partnership with those [Russia and China] and other countries...." The document also reiterates Trump's commitment to oppose regime change, stating, "We understand that the American way of life cannot be imposed on others, nor is it the inevitable culmination of progress." She identified the divergent points of emphasis as indications of an ongoing internal battle, noting that Trump recently had a very successful trip to China, and has spoken repeatedly of his "great" personal relationship with China's President Xi, while he has also had several recent very productive discussions with Putin.

Geopolitics Means War

The confrontational language in the report echoes comments of former top Obama officials CIA Director John Brennan and Director of National Intelligence James Clapper, who were part of the "Get Trump" team from the outset, signing on to the infamous, still unsubstantiated so-called "intelligence community assessment" of Jan. 7, 2017, that concluded, "with high confidence," that Russia meddled in the U.S. presidential campaign. On leaving their posts, both continued to attack Trump as naive for believing he can work with Russia.

In Australia, on June 7, 2017, Clapper claimed that it is in Russia's "genes to be opposed, diametrically opposed, to the United States and Western democracies." The two joined forces again on CNN's "State of the Union" program on November 12, 2017, to slam Trump and Russia. Brennan said that Trump is "intimidated" by Putin, and that Russia is "a threat to our democracy." Clapper chimed in, adding that "Putin is committed to undermining our system," and that Trump, by rejecting that view, "poses a peril to this country."

At the same time the National Security Strategy document was released, *Newsweek* magazine ran a cover story in its December 21 issue with the headline, "Putin is Preparing for World War III." The article has the usual Fake News characterization of Putin as a paranoid authoritarian dictator who uses the threat of encirclement and war to cover up for his economic failures. For example, it states that the Kremlin is mobilizing because "it is convinced war is imminent." It includes a quote from a former British Ambassador to Russia (who, naturally, wishes to remain anonymous), who said "Russia is engaged in

Tank unit, Russian Zapad 2017 exercise.

a strange sort of unilateral arms race."

This attempt to scare its readers is not a new tactic by *Newsweek*. In Aug. 2016 it reported, "Europeans Are Quietly Preparing for War with Russia."

An even more hysterical fantasy appeared in the German mass tabloid *Bild Zeitung* on December 20, which cited two unnamed NATO officials who charged that Russia's Zapad 2017 military exercise was a rehearsal for a full scale Russian military assault on Europe. According to this story, the Russians plan to occupy the three Baltic states, while attacking by air key infrastructure in Germany, Sweden and Finland. The two latter nations are being pushed hard to play a more active role in NATO. The article says the goal of Russia in launching such an attack is to paralyze NATO, while preventing reinforcements in the East. This article appears as there is a concerted effort to boost defense spending in Europe, along with the promotion of a European Union "defense union."

Mueller Under Seige

The move toward more aggressive war propaganda in the Trans-Atlantic region comes at a point when the Mueller witch-hunt is being seriously undermined by exposes of corruption within its ranks. The revelations of the role of top FBI Counterintelligence official, Peter Strzok, are particularly damaging, as they demonstrate conclusively that Strzok is at the center of a "web of corruption" which includes the highest levels of British intelligence, the Clinton campaign, and the FBI. The effort to contain the damage by supporters of Mueller, by belittling the evidence of corruption as a "conspiracy theory," fell apart last week, as Congressional Republicans have become emboldened in questioning leading FBI offi-

Special Counsel Robert Mueller (left) with some of his cabal of government officials or former officials: (left to right) Bruce Ohr, Deputy Associate Attorney General, Nellie Ohr, high-level intelligence consultant, and FBI agent Peter Strzok.

cials. Emerging in ongoing Congressional hearings is a picture that shows that Strzok was brought into the operation begun by James Comey, Clapper and Brennan, to smear Trump with allegations that he was in a conspiracy with Putin to become President. Comey's team, with Strzok at its head, was engaged in the smear campaign to prevent Trump from winning the election.

As we have reported, the most damning evidence is a text message sent by Strzok to his mistress, FBI lawyer Lisa Page, which was discovered by the Inspector General of the Department of Justice (DOJ). In the message, Strzok wrote to Page on Aug. 15, 2016: "I want to believe the path you threw out for consideration in Andy's office that there's no way Trump gets elected, but I'm afraid we can't take that risk. It's like an insurance policy...." "Andy's office" refers to Deputy FBI Director Andrew McCabe, a close ally of the Clinton political machine—meaning that the FBI hierarchy was directly involved in a scheme to sink Trump's campaign; the "insurance policy" obviously referred to using the Russiagate story, which was just then being developed by Strzok's team, to remove Trump, should he win the election!

It was at this same time that Strzok and other top FBI officials were brought into collaboration with "former" MI6 official Christopher Steele, who produced a dossier alleging that Putin had sexual blackmail material against Trump. Steele's dossier, produced for the Fusion GPS "opposition research" company, was funded by the Clinton campaign, likely with full backing from leading elements of British intelligence, whose GCHQ had begun tracking Trump in the summer of 2015, long before he laid waste to a field of 17 Republican opponents. Despite more than a year of attempts to corroborate Steele's allegations, McCabe admitted, in part through not answering questions in a Congressional hearing, that they have not been able to do it!

At left: Andrew McCabe, Deputy Director of the FBI.

Inset: Rep. Jim Jordan, Ohio.

There are many other pieces to this story, including Strzok's role in exonerating Clinton for her use of a private server, his role in the set-up which led to Michael Flynn's guilty plea to a single count of "lying to the FBI," and top DOJ official Bruce Ohr's meeting(s) with Steele, while his wife was employed by Fusion GPS. These are coming out due to the work of Republican Congressmen, with more hearings to come. A sample of some of the responses from Congressional investigators to these revelations, gives a flavor of how things are turning against Mueller's prosecutorial thuggery and the FBI's systemic corruption.

On Dec.18, Rep. Trey Gowdy (R-South Carolina) responded to the Strzok revelations by saying that the anti-Trump messages sent back-and-forth with his mistress show an "unprecedented" level of bias. "It is devastating" that they spoke of developing an " 'insurance policy' in case Donald Trump won. What I hope is that insurance policy was not a counterintelligence investigation into the Trump campaign. This was a level of bias that you rarely see."

Rep. Devin Nunes (R-California), chair of the House Intelligence Committee, followed his committee hearings by asking, "I hate to use the word corrupt, but they've become at least so dirty that who's watching the watchmen? Who's investigating these people? There is no one."

Rep. Jim Jordan (R-Ohio), who has been demanding subpoenas be issued so that all those involved can be interrogated, is especially focused on the Steele dossier, and whether it was used to obtain warrants from the secret FISA Court to conduct surveillance on the Trump campaign. In reviewing the role of Strzok and Ohr, he said, "Everything points to the fact that there was an orchestrated plan to try to prevent Donald Trump from becoming the President of the United States."

Florida Rep. Matt Gaetz, who recently spoke directly to Trump about what has been turned up involving "conflicts of interest" and "outright corruption," said "…it's time for Bob Mueller to put up or shut up. If there's evidence of collusion, let's see it." He said, in reference to the meeting in "Andy's office," that it is disgusting that a "bunch of bureaucrats can sit around and scheme about how to deprive the American people of their duly elected President."

Illegal Seizure of Transition Emails

One other element of Mueller's prosecutorial fraud came to light last week, which was his team's seizure of tens of thousands of emails from Trump's transition team, despite the legal ruling by the General Counsel for the General Services Administration (GSA), Richard Beckler, that these were private, and should remain in the hands of the GSA. When Beckler was hospitalized, Mueller's operatives seized the records, without receiving a court-approved subpoena. Shortly after his hospitalization, Beckler died.

The seizure of these documents was the subject of a biting op-ed by constitutional scholar Jonathan Turley in *The Hill* of December 18. Turley, who is no fan of Trump, nevertheless correctly identified Mueller's action as "legally unprecedented and strategically reckless," warning that the use of "tainted" evidence could lead to the overturning of any conviction that Mueller might get. Turley described this as an abuse of law, following in the footsteps of the notorious former FBI Director J. Edgar Hoover, writing that "Hoover's attitude toward the use of federal power lingers [within the FBI] like a dormant virus. Too often investigators interpret uncertain legal questions as a license for action." Turley specifically identified Mueller's lead prosecutor Andrew Weissman, as one whose record includes "major reversals in past prosecutions for exceeding the scope of the criminal code or [engaging in] questionable ethical conduct."

Turley's comments, along with those of former judge and prosecutor, Fox News legal commentator Jeanine Pirro, represent a sharp break into the open in major media, reflecting the turn against Mueller's operations. Pirro called Mueller's team a "criminal cabal," which should be taken out in "cuffs" (handcuffs). They are acting as a "core group of arrogant, corrupt and lawless individuals that felt that they, and not we, should decide a presidential election."

As these quotes from Congressmen and legal experts show, there is now finally a willingness to break through the cover-up and get at the truth about Russiagate—that it has been a story concocted, from the beginning, with no evidence, to either contain Trump, or get rid of him, in defense of an old crumbling order, and that the real "meddling" in the election by a foreign country came from Britain, in coordination with the Clinton campaign and the FBI. But that is not enough. It is now time that the deeper issue behind Russiagate be exposed, and that issue is the unwillingness of the promoters of the neocon unilateral world order to give up their power. The endless wars and endless bailouts they have imposed are necessary for them to keep the world embroiled in deadly, useless geopolitical conflicts, which inflict misery on the majority of the world's people, while allowing them to loot with impunity.

Donald Trump's election victory showed that the American people were tired of this immoral, bankrupt order. Now, citizens must mobilize to shut down Russiagate, to free Trump to bring the United States into the New Paradigm of cooperation and development initiated by President Xi Jinping of China, with full support from Russia's President Putin. The era of geopolitics must be brought to an end, if the annihilation of mankind is to be prevented. Shutting down the Mueller investigation, and jailing the corrupt officials behind it, would be a good first step in that direction. Toward that end, LaRouchePAC activists delivered this week, to every U.S. House and Senate office and to many committee staffers, the report which first exposed Russiagate as a fraud, "Robert Mueller Is an Immoral Legal Assassin." As Lyndon LaRouche commented, "the gate has been opened"—it is now the time to move!

Houston's Mayor Leads Trade Mission to China

by Brian Lantz

Dec. 22—Repercussions and opportunities arising from President Trump's November visit to China and his discussions with Chinese President Xi Jinping continue to unfold, as new agreements on trade and investment become reality. Already, at the conclusion of the Presidential visit, an announcement was made that as part of the $250 billion of investments signed during that visit, the Chinese firm China Energy Investment Corporation would invest $83.7 billion in shale gas development and chemical manufacturing projects in the state of West Virginia, over two decades. Following up on these agreements, between December 2 and 9, Houston Mayor Sylvester Turner led Houston's largest-ever trade delegation in a visit to China, for eight days of discussions with Chinese business and government leaders. Joined by seventy businessmen, as well as local elected officials and community leaders, the Turner delegation traveled to Beijing, Shenzhen and Shanghai.

houstontx.gov

Mayor Sylvester Turner (fifth from left) with Houston's largest ever trade delegation to a foreign country, shown here in China.

The potential ramifications of these developments are enormous. West Virginia is one of the poorest of America's states, with high unemployment and escalating rates of death from drug addiction and suicide. The Houston metropolitan area was devastated by Hurricane Harvey, and is still reeling from the continuing effects of that catastrophe. The immediate tangible reality is that the agreements that have already been reached on Chinese investment in Texas and West Virginia will put people back to work and result in major industrial and scientific projects in those areas.

Additionally, an even greater potential has been revealed by these agreements, one whereby a nation-wide economic renaissance and a rebuilding of America's productive industrial and scientific capabilities could be realized, were the United States to join with China and other nations as a full partner in the "win-win" policy of the global Belt and Road Initiative. Were the United States to fully jettison the geopolitical Obama-era policy of military and strategic confrontation with China—as President Trump has repeatedly stated is his personal goal—a new era of peace and an in-depth rebuilding of America's productive economy becomes realizable.

What the Houston Team Accomplished

Immediately upon the Houston delegation's return, the Houston Mayor's Office released a Dec. 11 statement on the outcome of the mission to China. The press release opens, "Backed by Houston's largest-ever trade delegation to a foreign country, Mayor Sylvester Turner declared after meetings with government officials and business leaders in China last week that Houston and the world's most populous nation have reached 'a golden moment' of mutual economic advantage."

Here are highlights of the Houston trade mission, many of which are noted in the Mayor's Office release. The potentials are enormous:

• The Mayor and delegation members met with Li Pumin, secretary general of China's National Development and Reform Commission (NDRC). "Some of the most compelling statements made by Chinese officials in meetings with the mayor came from Li Pumin," says the release. The NDRC, which works directly under the State Council, studies and formulate policies for the economic and social development of China. For their "Healthy China Strategy," Li Pumin said, "China needs a medical center like the Texas Medical Center," and was already utilizing Houston's medical institutions for help in meeting the growing healthcare requirements of its 1.3 billion people. "The market will have a leading role and the government will give it support," Li added, according to the Mayor's Office press release.

Why the Texas Medical Center? The Texas Medical Center is the largest medical complex in the world. It contains 54 medicine-related institutions, with 21 hospitals and eight specialty institutions, eight academic and research institutions, four medical schools and seven nursing schools. The 50-million-square-foot TMC serves over ten million patients a year, and employs over 100,000 people, including 20,000 physicians, scientists, researchers and other advanced-degree professionals in the life sciences. All 54 institutions are not-for-profit. Its schools and facilities train thousands of new doctors and other health professionals every year, and interface with NASA's Human Spaceflight Programs and Houston's Johnson Space Center.

• In Shenzhen, a Houston "Sister City" (since 1986) and actually the first leg of the delegation's visit, an MOU (Memorandum of Understanding) was signed between the Houston Airport System and the Chinese company CIMC (China International Marine Containers). "Houston and our airport system have the infrastructure to accommodate CIMC-TianDa as it seeks a platform to compete for business across the Americas," Mayor

Houston Mayor Turner (left), calls the signing of an economic memorandum with Beijing Mayor Chen Jining, a "golden moment" of mutual economic advantage.

Turner said. "Our air cargo facilities, combined with our port system, provide the logistics infrastructure to support the development, manufacturing and transport of large-scale equipment wherever world markets take them. We believe the jobs this business would create represent a good growth opportunity for Houston." CIMC-TianDa, a subsidiary of CIMC, which specializes in airport and seaport equipment design, development, manufacturing and maintenance, is seeking a facility to support operations in the Western Hemisphere, and the MOU involves a real estate lease or purchase options at or near George Bush Intercontinental Airport. While the initial number of Houston-area jobs to be created would be small, future prospects would be big.

• In Shanghai, the Wison Group welcomed Houston's trade and investment mission at the company's headquarters in Zhangjiang, Pudong Province. Mr. Song Qu, President of Wison Group, greeted the delegations, and Mr. Qingguo Jiang, Wison Vice President, briefed the business delegation, led by Bob Harvey of the Greater Houston Partnership, on the company. Wison is an engineering, procurement, and construction company, or EPC firm. It is currently contracted with Taiwan's Formosa Plastic in the building of chemical plants in Comfort, TX, southwest of Houston. In July, "Wison Engineering was awarded an engineering, procurement, fabrication and construction contract for Formosa Plastics U.S.A.'s newly-built Low Density Polyethylene plant in Texas, while Wison Offshore & Marine has taken on the module fabrication work scope. This very project signified Wison is gaining market recognition in the U.S. market, which paved the way for its growth in North America," according to a Wison press release. Wison has been contracted to "engineer, procure, construct, install, and commission" the world's first "floating LNG liquefaction, re-gasification, and storage unit" off the coast of Colombia. Wison also formed a consortium with Korea's Hyundai Engineering & Construction Co. to sign a contract with PDSVA, Venezuela's state-owned oil company, to expand PDVSA's Puerto la Cruz refinery.

Also in Shanghai, Mayor Turner and members of the delegation met with Xu Kunlin, vice-mayor of Shanghai. Xu Kunlin said Shanghai and Houston have had friendly ties for a long time and became sister cities in 2015. A Shanghai government press release reported, "In keeping with the requirements by the central authorities, Shanghai is building, at full steam, the China (Shanghai) Pilot Free Trade Zone and a science and technology innovation hub with a global reach. Mayor Xu Kunlin welcomed Houston companies to be a part of all this and hoped the Houston mayor's visit will further boost the friendly exchange and cooperation between the two cities. Also, the Shanghai vice-mayor extended an invitation to the Houston businesses to attend the first China International Import Expo to be held in Shanghai in November, 2018."

• Oil and LNG exports through the expanded Panama Canal are now looked to as part of a "quick fix" to boost the weakened economies of Texas and Louisiana. So it was significant that Mayor Turner and delegation members met with Lui Baowue, the vice administrator of China's National Energy Administration. Mayor Turner was told that China is looking to Houston's relatively young liquefied natural gas export industry to help China triple its use of natural gas by 2020 as it reduces its use of coal to lessen air pollution. He also reported that China was on the verge of tapping Houston energy company expertise in developing China's shale potential.

• According to the Houston Mayor's Office statement, "The trade talks became even more focused" as the delegation met with Wang Xiandong, a top executive of the construction giant China Civil Engineering Construction Corporation (CCECC). Wang Xiandong said "presentations by the Mayor and Greater Houston Partnership President Bob Harvey made it more likely his organization will set up a business base in Houston." The Houston Mayor's statement recognizes that CCECC "represents engineering firms that provide massive services across the globe, especially in developing countries in Africa and other continents." CCECC, set up under China's State Council in 1979, undertakes numerous key projects including railways, highways, bridges, buildings, and municipal works around the world. Wang Xiandong has himself served as a manager of CCECC projects in Africa. This could potentially be a major contribution to building out a new infrastructure platform for the Untied Sates. CCECC already has a developing capability for training and employing the local labor force, and for technology-transfer.

• Mayor Turner and delegation members also met with Bank of China Executive Vice President Yingxin Gao to pursue the possibility of establishing a banking branch in Houston. The Bank of China is one of China's "Big Four" commercial banks, with offices around the world, including New York City. The Industrial and Commercial Bank of China (ICBC)—another "Big Four" bank—just opened offices in Houston in October. With Glass-Steagall reforms and a return to national banking and national credit in the United States (aspects of Lyndon LaRouche's "Four Laws"), the potential exists for major long-term credit generation, to jointly create the financing for desperately needed major projects, including the required hurricane and flood control/water management infrastructure needed along the entire Gulf Coast.

• Also in China's capital, Beijing, Mayor Turner and the delegation met with Beijing Mayor Chen Jining. Mayor Chen stated that the Houston delegation's presentations gave the city of Houston a higher business profile in China. "The importance and the potential of the city of Houston has been undervalued [in China], so as per your suggestion, we hope to strengthen our relationship," Mayor Chen told Mayor Turner.

Mayor Turner summed up, "We are in a golden moment where Houston is the uniquely positioned supplier of goods and services that China needs to meet the growing demands of its booming nation as its president, Xi Jinping, spurs his nation to increase its interactions with the rest of world. Expanded trade with China—already our second largest international trade partner—brings more jobs and more investment capital to Houston."

The lesson to be learned here is that what has been accomplished by the Houston trade delegation, as well as by the earlier visit of President Trump, including the $250 billion in investments that were agreed to, represent only the "tip of the iceberg" of what is possible—what might be accomplished with full U.S. participation in the Belt and Road. This is how geopolitics ends and a future of cooperative economic development begins.

CHRISTMAS CONCERT, DEC. 16

Beethoven at Co-Cathedral of St. Joseph

The following are the welcoming remarks by Lynn Yen, Executive Director of The Foundation for the Revival of Classical Culture at the Brooklyn, New York concert.

Good afternoon! On behalf of the Foundation for the Revival of Classical Culture I want to thank you all for coming to the concert. We want to thank the Co-Cathedral of St. Joseph, and Monsignor Harrington, for allowing us to hold today's event, on the birthday of the composer Ludwig van Beethoven, who was born in the year 1770, six years before our Declaration of Independence, 247 years ago.

Beethoven's *Ninth Symphony* is often played around the world at this time of year, because of its theme of universal brotherhood. It has also often been used as an anthem of freedom, as it was when the Berlin Wall fell in November of 1989. Beethoven takes his words from the German poet Friedrich Schiller: "*Alle Menschen werden Bruder*" ("All men shall be brothers.") There is also the message:

Ihr stürtz nieder, Millionen?
Ahnest du den Schöpfer, Welt?
Such ihn über 'm Sternenzelt!
Über Sternen muss er wohnen.

You stumble, millions?
Do you sense the Creator, world?
Seek Him above the starry canopy!
Above the stars He must dwell.

Beethoven did not have a very happy childhood.

Ilko Dimov

Beethoven also began losing his hearing in his mid-twenties. Imagine! For a musician, hearing is almost as important as breathing. Beethoven, in despair, even once considered taking his own life, but fought back. He used his loss of hearing as a challenge for his musical creativity, as an aid to his own journey of spiritual discovery. His greatest music, including the sections of the *Mass in C Major* you will hear today, was composed in the shadow of his deafness. Finally, when completely deaf, he composed, and rejoiced, in his *Ninth Symphony*.

In New York City today, many young people are forced to live through childhoods and adolescences of deprivation. One out of every ten of our public high school students is homeless. There are other difficulties which they endure, and those difficulties are, like Beethoven's deafness, unsought and undeserved. At Christmas, when the saving power of one unique child is the focus of the entire Western world, and much of the world besides, the power of music provides a gateway leading to the inner experience of self-transformation that must happen in America and the world in order that we rid the Earth of what President John Kennedy called the common enemies of man—"tyranny, poverty, famine and war itself."

Young people are the natural heralds of that new era of true humanity. Those are the people that Beethoven said that he was writing his music for—the yet-unborn millions that he addressed in his *Ninth Symphony*.

Today we need a universal chorus, comprising people from all over the world. You can assemble that right here in Brooklyn and Queens from out of our school system! Our Foundation endorses the project that the Schiller Institute has so far been leading to recruit 1,500 people in our city to that chorus. We urge all of you to join that chorus, and to support the growth of that chorus.

We believe that the power of Classical music is only truly experienced when it is presented from the standpoint of the immortality of the human soul, as a life and death mission, to say something to the millions yet unborn, to the future, that will never die.

Please enjoy this afternoon's concert, but also consider seriously the message behind it, and the season that we now celebrate. Thank you!

DEC. 16 SCHILLER INSTITUTE CONCERT PROGRAM NOTES

Beethoven's 'New Song,' The Mass in C Major, Op. 86

by Dennis Speed

"Man can think a poem and write it…He can think a symphony and compose it… He can think of a great civilization and produce it. He can be a Handel moving into the highest heavens and transcribing the glad thunders and gentle sighings of the great Messiah. By his ability to reason, his power and memory, and his gift of imagination, man transcends time and space. As marvelous as are the stars, as great as is Handel's Messiah… is the mind of the man that studies them."

—Dr. Martin Luther King, Jr.

"Prince, what you are, you are by accident of birth; what I am, I am through my own efforts. There have been thousands of princes, and will be thousands more; there is only one Beethoven!"
—According to tradition, from a letter which Beethoven wrote to Prince Lichnowsky, when the latter attempted to persuade him to play for some French officers on his estate in Silesia.

The month of December commemorates, among other saints, Saint Ambrose (340-397), Bishop of Milan who, together with the mother of St. Augustine, was central to converting Augustine to Christianity. Augustine (354-430) reported that it was not merely the eloquence of Ambrose's preaching, but his hymns that were essential in reaching Augustine's heart. Ambrose, the author of the still-performed "Veni Redemptor Gentium" and many other hymns, and later Augustine, regarded music as an essential "divining rod" for the soul, a compass pointing the believer in the direction of the highest good. The theological basis for their outlook was stated two centuries earlier by St. Clement of Alexandria (150-211/215): "The Lord fashioned man a beautiful, breathing instrument, after His own image; and assuredly He Himself is an all-harmonious instrument of God, melodious and holy, the wisdom that is above this world, the heavenly Word … Because the Word was from the first. He was and is the divine beginning of all things; but because He lately took a name,— the name consecrated of old and worthy of power, the Christ,—I have called Him a New Song."

Augustine's book-length Platonic dialogue, *De Musica*, upshifted the world's and Western Civilization's musical practice. In its discussion and distinction of the difference between the "numbers of the flesh" and the "numbers of the mind," the idea of "divine proportion" was made increasingly intelligible. It would not be until the work of Johannes Kepler (1571-1630), Gottfried Wilhelm Leibniz (1646-1716), and J.S. Bach (1685-1750) that the system of well-tempered polyphony would provide a language and musical practice capable of illustrating the "New Song" of which the second century's Clement had spoken. Bach, Haydn, Mozart and Beethoven would all choose the liturgy and sequencing of the Mass, in its various settings (Requiem, Solemn High Mass, and Masses for certain feast days) as a special point of intervention into the culture of their times. Their contributions required them to act often as the internal voice of the liturgy, such that the meaning behind and above the oft-repeated words of the Mass was experienced afresh by the congregants and the clergy as well, demonstrating the unbounded possibility for musical expression offered by the sacred text.

'Man, Help Yourself! For Ye Are Able!'

The *Mass in C Major* of Ludwig van Beethoven, written in 1807, is rarely performed in its entirety, and deserves to be heard far more frequently. For those unfamiliar with Beethoven's profoundly religious view of the world, the Mass will help to dispel the idea of Beethoven as an "Enlightenment intellectual" or "indifferent practitioner of the Catholic faith." His 1803 *Christ On The Mount of Olives*, a composition that concentrates on the story of the agony in the garden at Gethsemane, was his first major religious composition for chorus and orchestra, written just after his successful battle against the temptation to commit suicide in response to his loss of hearing, documented in his 1802 "Heiligenstadt Testament."

In the small town of Heiligenstadt, just outside of Vienna, in the Summer of 1802 Beethoven had written the most personal of letters to explain his attempts to cope with his increasing deafness, noticed by him in the 1790s, when he was in his mid-to-late 20s. "Oh! ye who think or declare me to be hostile, morose, and misanthropical, how unjust you are, and how little you know the secret cause of what appears thus to you! My heart and mind were ever from childhood prone to the most tender feelings of affection, and I was always disposed to accomplish something great. But you must remember that six years ago I was attacked by an incurable malady, aggravated by unskillful physicians, deluded from year to year, too, by the hope of relief, and at length forced to the conviction of a lasting affliction (the cure of which may go on for years, and perhaps after all prove impracticable)...."

Though he indeed briefly contemplated suicide, Beethoven overcame the seduction of his despair. He says, in his Testament: "But what humiliation when any one beside me heard a flute in the far distance, while I heard nothing, or when others heard a shepherd singing, and I still heard nothing! Such things brought me to the verge of desperation, and well-nigh caused me to put an end to my life. Art! art alone deterred me. Ah! how could I possibly quit the world before bringing forth all that I felt it was my vocation to produce?... Perhaps I shall get better; perhaps not, I am ready.... Forced to become a philosopher already in my twenty-eighth year, oh it is not easy, and for the artist much more difficult than for anyone else.... Divine One, Thou seest my inmost soul, and thou knowest that therein dwells the love of mankind and the desire to do good."

His "good works," including his late string quartets, his piano sonatas, his opera *Fidelio*, his Ninth Symphony and *Missa Solemnis*, many of them written when he was completely deaf, comprise a "New Testament" of human thought, composed not out of bitterness toward, but love for the mankind of the future, and the universe as a whole. Doing good, and the desire to do good, is the only efficient recourse available to an individual or a society as a means to correct the willful, deliberate commission of evil. Choosing to do good rather than evil is the only true act of atonement. The act of self-redemption of mankind through giving one's life for all humanity, is an act of universal love (Agape), the subject of the "Christ Mass," or Christmas. Beethoven's *Mass in C Major* allows those not of the Christian faith, or of any faith, as well as believers, to discover the true marvel of the universal message behind and above the words of the text. A dialogue offered by the composer with the heart of the listener, allows the mind of the listener to be freshly engaged, beyond the obstacles of unfamiliarity or pre-judgement. This, the Mass, properly performed and properly tuned, can be as accessible to people today, no matter their background, as it was when it was written 210 years ago.

Such musical/spiritual experiences are increasingly important to facilitate the newly emerging possibility of a dialogue among all the world's nations. For example, China, in its proposal for world dialogue through creating a "New Silk Road," now recalls to us the days of the Italian Renaissance. Then, scholars of the Church such as Cardinal Nicholas of Cusa, and his scientific collaborators including the architect Filippo Brunelleschi and the astronomer Paolo Toscanelli, pursued a new pathway of understanding and reconciliation of peoples, both through the 1439 Council of Florence, and through individual contact with scholars and thinkers from the whole known (and even unknown) world. This new dialogue is notable for the opportunity it provides for the correction of centuries-old evils, committed by nations, elites, and individuals against the human race.

This principle of dialogue should be very familiar to Catholics from the work, in the late 70s, 80s, 90s and until 2005, of Saint John Paul II. Pope Saint John Paul II's famous pilgrimages of atonement, in which he publicly apologized for the historical transgressions committed by members of the Church against other nations and faiths, were also accompanied by many encyclicals and pastoral messages, including *Laborem Exercens*

Full Schiller Institute Chorus in Co-Cathedral of St. Joseph in Brooklyn, N.Y.

and *Centissimus Annus*, in which he outlined a philosophical orientation toward a human, non-predatory form of "human good works," including in physical economy. In Part II, section 6 of *Laborem Exercens*, we are instructed: "Man has to subdue the earth and dominate it, because as the 'image of God' he is a person, that is to say, a subjective being capable of acting in a planned and rational way, capable of deciding about himself, and with a tendency to self-realization. As a person, man is therefore the subject of work. As a person he works, he performs various actions belonging to the work process; independently of their objective content, these actions must all serve to realize his humanity, to fulfill the calling to be a person that is his by reason of his very humanity."

Beethoven recognized that it was through the subduing of his own nature—of his understandable despair at losing the most precious gift that a musician has, which is his hearing—that he became capable of hearing from within, more perfectly than he had physically heard before. The works which were to come, including his *Missa Solemnis*, his Ninth Symphony and his late string quartets, were composed in total deafness, and yet are still unsurpassed in their profundity and their humanity. The inscription written by him at the top of the third movement of his Quartet in A minor Op. 132: "*Heiliger Dankgesang eines Genesenen an die Gottheit in der lydischen Tonart*" ("Holy song of thanks to God from a convalescent in the Lydian mode"), removes all doubt of his clarity of view as to the source and purpose of his life in music.

The Foundation for the Revival of Classical Culture and the Schiller Institute NYC Chorus are particularly committed to acquainting, over the course of the next year, the New York area audience with this work of Beethoven, performing it at the "Verdi tuning" of C=256, and doing so in the context of other sacred texts, including, in this instance, the "Christmas" portion of Handel's *Messiah*, and African-American Spirituals. Conductor John Sigerson is offering a series of lectures on the theme, "Beethoven As A Physical Scientist." Sigerson is the co-author of a *Manual on Registration and Tuning*, which has sought to restore the primacy of the human voice, and voice-placement, as the origin of all truly Classical compositions, whatever their form. The re-situating of the scientific, as well as artistic breakthroughs surrounding Beethoven's unique use of Bach's well-tempered system, by demonstrating the principles of proper tuning through choral music designed to celebrate the infinite creative potential of the human mind, is indeed a "New Song" for these culturally troubled times.

Choral director and Schiller Institute New York Chorus Founder Diane Sare's selection of African-American Spirituals, and "O Come, O Come Emmanuel," which open tonight's program, continues a practice that the Schiller Institute began some years ago, thanks to the influence of musicians Sylvia Olden Lee and William Warfield. Both were active as board members of the Institute until their deaths in 2004 and 2002, respectively. Whenever the Schiller chorus performs, the repertoire of our concerts is always selected to invoke the high standards demanded by these great musicians, who were masters of the entirety of the Classical repertoire. But they also demanded truth, and the truth is that the African-American Spiritual belongs here, together with Bach and Beethoven, because of what those songs say to mankind, in the same thoughts, if not the same words, as the liturgy of the Mass.

Christmas Concert on Beethoven's Birthday in Brooklyn

by Diane Sare

Dec. 25—On Saturday, Dec. 16, over 500 people attended a Christmas concert presented by the Foundation for the Revival of Classical Culture, and featuring a combined chorus of over 100 voices, including the Schiller Institute NYC Chorus, and members of Schiller Institute Choruses from Boston, Leesburg, Va., and Baltimore. The concert included parts of Beethoven's Mass in C, as well as excerpts of Handel's *Messiah*, and other selections. This is the fourth concert that the Schiller choruses have participated in at the Co-Cathedral of St. Joseph in Brooklyn, including a presentation of the Mozart *Requiem* embedded within an actual Requiem Mass, performed on Sunday September 11, 2016, in honor of the firemen of Brooklyn's Ladder Company 105, and all victims of 9/11.

Monsignor Kieran Harrington of the Co-Cathedral began the program with a welcome to all, invoking the responsibility for the whole human race as well as the promise of a new beginning associated with Christmas. He was followed by remarks from the Foundation for the Revival of Classical Culture's Executive Director, Lynn Yen, who discussed Beethoven's triumph over adversity, the courage required today to triumph over adversity with beauty. The concert program began with three songs, all directed by Diane Sare: "O, Come, O Come, Emmanuel" (arranged by Sare), "Ain'a that Good News" (Dawson), and "Glory. Glory, Glory To the Newborn King" (Hogan). This was followed by the Kyrie, Gloria, and Credo from Beethoven's Mass in C, and most of the Christmas section of Handel's *Messiah*, directed by John Sigerson.

The chorus was joined by distinguished artists Robert Wilson, on piano, and soloists Indira Mahajan, soprano; Linda Childs, alto; Everett Suttle, tenor; and

Ilko Dimov

Full Schiller Institute Chorus in Co-Cathedral of St. Joseph in Brookly, N.Y.

Jay Baylon, bass-baritone.

For two weekends prior to the concert, a small sub-section of the chorus had gone out to sing Christmas Carols in front of the Metropolitan Museum of Art. What struck the singers was the hunger of the population for beauty. People were particularly responsive to carols like "Silent Night," "Hark, the Herald Angels Sing," and "Lo, How a Rose E'er Blooming," and as long as they were sung well, large crowds would gather. A handful of people jumped in to join the singing. Many were seen wiping their eyes in tears of joy. At least one of the people met there attended the concert, and signed up to join the chorus in the new season.

Also indicative of the thirst for beauty, and probably of the dramatic improvement of the chorus over its three years of existence, is that many people brought others. In addition to the spirited effort of our intrepid "Manhattan Project" organizers, who distributed leaflets, attended events, etc., 35 or more chorus members sold tickets to their friends and family. A number of young people were brought by their parents—small children and teenagers as well, who sat in rapt attention listening to the music.

In one case, a small boy, perhaps about three or four years of age, was told by his parents that it was time to go, although the concert was not quite over. As his parents headed to the doors, he ran back to the pew where they had been sitting and held on to the back of it tightly as the chorus began singing. A bystander tapped the boy on the shoulder, and he did not even notice, so intense was his concentration on the music!

A woman met just the week before at an event at the church, and who heads up an organizing committee on behalf of canonization for the priest who built the first orphanage for African-American children in New York (which was then burned down twice by the Ku Klux Klan), organized nine other people to attend the concert!

A Chinese-American member of the chorus succeeded in getting a prominent short announcement into a Chinese-language newspaper, which resulted in several people making the two-hour trek by subway to come from Flushing to Brooklyn.

Another couple from Staten Island who are very active in Italian organizations attended. They had been met at a hearing in Staten Island about the Columbus statue where the wife testified. She explained that they always attend another service in Manhattan, but decided to come to the concert and were very happy with their decision. Other people, as they were leaving, commented on a similar circumstance of having to choose from multiple events, deciding on our Christmas concert.

Several people, including the video crew, commented on the clarity and transparency of the soloists, as well as the chorus. This was probably a result of the Verdi proper tuning, which a couple of musicians in the audience remarked on.

Twenty-three people signed sheets expressing interest in joining one of the Schiller Institute NYC chorus chapters. The enthusiastic response to this performance, which was not technically perfect at every moment (although quite solid overall), must be attributed to something more than the Verdi tuning, or the bel canto technique stressed by the directors. What came across from beginning to end, including in the remarks of the Monsignor, those of Lynn Yen, and the program notes, as well as the singing, is *intent*, the dedication to what Friedrich Schiller called the aesthetical education of Man. In a world where our minds are assaulted daily by pornography and violence labelled "news," it is only human to demand something better reflecting the dignity of mankind.

The Foundation for the Revival of Classical Culture and the Schiller Institute NYC Chorus are planning to perform the full Beethoven Mass in C, in a concert on April 4, right after Easter and in honor of Dr. Martin Luther King, Jr, on the occasion of the 50th anniversary of the tragedy of his assassination.

Diane Sare conducting.

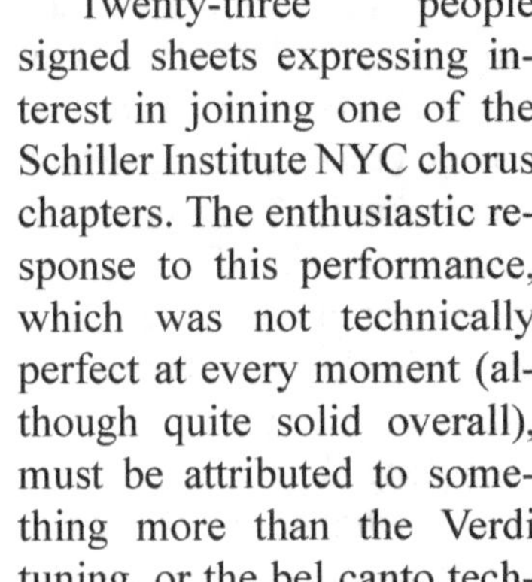

Soloists

Detroit and LaRouche's Fourth Law

by Susan Kokinda

Dec. 24—There is a deep resonance with Lyndon La-Rouche's "machine-tool-principle" in the blue-collar, Midwestern states which delivered the Presidency to Donald Trump in 2016. The desire to build and produce is still beating in the hearts of men and women in places like Michigan and Ohio, despite the downward spiral which has gripped the region and the nation since the assassination of President John Kennedy. But the *science* of how to create a society which will durably build and produce into the future, and which can protect itself from the evil policies of deindustrialization and dehumanization, is lacking, not only in the population, but in the Presidency itself.

Harrison Schmidt, last American Lunar Mission, Apollo 17.

Missing is the conscious principle which defines mankind and which must define the basis for a society's decisions, economic or otherwise. In his seminal 2014 paper, "Four New Laws to Save the U.S.A. Now! Not an Option: An Immediate Necessity," Lyndon La-Rouche asserts that principle as the basis of his fourth law:

"The knowable measure, in principle, of the difference between man and all among the lower forms of life, is found in what has been usefully regarded as the naturally upward evolution of the human species, in contrast to all other known categories of living species. The standard of measurement of these compared relationships, is that mankind is enabled to evolve upward, and that categorically, by those voluntarily no‰tic powers of the human individual will."

In a Detroit suburb, leaders and members of the Midwest LaRouche movement explored that principle on Dec. 17 at a meeting entitled, "Fulfilling the Dreams of Mankind Or Why the British Empire Wants to Overthrow the President." The focus was the "noetic powers of the human individual will" as embodied in the revival of a space program and in the revival of a classical culture. The meeting was appropriately opened by excerpts from Mozart's *Eine Kleine Nachtmusik* played by a string quartet, organized by one of the leading activists in the area.

While the audience was expecting and did receive an update on the breaking developments around LaRouche PAC's successful exposure of the attempted Mueller-run coup against the President, they were told that this was not a political meeting, but rather a classical composition. LaRouche PAC Policy Committee member Bill Roberts said, "We are in the process of freeing the President from this coup; now we must also free the minds of the American people," so that, as Friedrich Schiller put it, a great moment in history does not find a little people.

Roberts focused his discussion on the need to restore a sense of mission for the nation, as had been embodied in the Kennedy space program and as is promised by President Trump in his Dec. 11 Oval Office announcement and Presidential Directive to return to the nation to the Moon and beyond. That announcement was made exactly 45 years ago to the day after the last American lunar mission, Apollo 17. In the Oval Office with the President was Apollo 17 as-

Diane Sare leading an early rehearsal of the NYC Community Chorus.

tronaut Harrison Schmitt, one of the last two Americans to walk on the Moon. Schmitt recently gave an interview to a New Mexico newspaper, in which he reflected on where the U.S. and mankind would be today, with an industrial base on the Moon and on the way to Mars, had President Kennedy not been assassinated.

"Man is mankind's only true measure of the history of our Solar system, and what reposes within it. That is the same thing, as the most honored meaning and endless achievement of the human species, now within nearby Solar space, heading upward to mastery over the Sun and its Solar system, the one discovered (uniquely, as a matter of fact), by Johannes Kepler."

Lyndon LaRouche, in "The Four Laws"

Rather than such a mission, our nation has been taken over by monetarism.

Roberts contrasted that loss of mission in the United States, to the sense of mission gripping "everyday people" in China, and showed an excerpt from a Chinese television documentary on the construction of the Hong Kong-Macao-Zhuhai bridge. That project, begun in 2009, now nearing completion, will be the longest in the world. The section of the video captured the thoughts of two young people, probably fresh out of college, who rose to the challenge and committed themselves to the eight-year-long project under admittedly difficult circumstances. It was clear that these young engineers had improved their own self-conception in order to accomplish something important for the future of the nation.

That provided an appropriate introduction to the main presentation—the video of Helga Zepp-LaRouche who had just visited Zhuhai, China and had had the opportunity to travel on the nearly-completed bridge. Mrs. Zepp-LaRouche was a keynote speaker at the Maritime Silk Road conference in Zhuhai, in China's Guangdong Province, on Nov. 29, and delivered a powerful speech on the classical principles which can and must unite all great civilizations. Participants were gripped by this very profound presentation, in which Helga Zepp-LaRouche demonstrated that man's ideas are commensurate with and can change the physical universe. When it was over, the musician-organizer quietly declared, "Helga rocks."

The audience was presented with two challenges. The first, to which all agreed—widespread dissemination of the Mueller dossier. The second challenge was and is more daunting and its actualization is a work-in-progress.

LaRouche PAC's Hector Villareal presented the urgent necessity of building a Detroit Schiller Institute chorus, modeled on the dramatic success of the Schiller Institute New York chorus:

Last year LaRouche PAC and the Schiller Institute moved on a challenge issued by Mr. LaRouche to build a chorus of citizens politically activated by our fight against the chaotic violence occurring in the country and the Obama

Administration's traitorous protection of the Anglo/Saudi funders of 9/11.

These citizens of New York were of course most deeply affected by the terrorist attack on 9/11. Yet the impact was felt all over the country. A young woman who perished in one of the flights had graduated at the same high school I went to.

So these deeply affected citizens were challenged to wage a fight for justice against the greatest sponsors of violence, sponsors of terrorism and aggressive warfare all over the world, the Anglo-American and Saudi financial apparatus. Although the particular fight focussed on the impeachment of Obama and declassification of the 28-page chapter from the original Joint Congressional Inquiry into 9-11, containing the truth of 9/11, this was not our only weapon in this fight.

Our main weapon was Mozart. Mr. LaRouche, in his unique genius, challenged people to not only fight for an issue or series of issues but rather to fight for their immortality. This is the subject of Mozart's *Requiem* which we performed in nearly every borough of New York City for the 15th anniversary 9/11 commemorations. Every individual's mortal life will inevitably perish. Thus the crucial subject is the immortality of the human soul.

Most people towards the end of their life begin to think about the well-being of their kids, the next generation and what they have done for them—what they have contributed to their betterment. This is ordinary, this is moral, but not extraordinary. Extraordinary is the person who fights for the UNIVERSAL betterment of mankind.

This is where classical culture and properly performed classical music comes in. It is designed not only to be sensually pleasing and beautiful. That is, beauty as Friederich Schiller defined it, as a process of human creative development which ennobles the human soul. Classical composition provides us an insight into this process of development and potential, and is that into which Mr. LaRouche is always fighting to give us an insight. That's why we sing.

Detroit used to sing—not Motown, but Mozart and

Grinnell Brothers Piano Factory, Detroit, Michigan.

Bach. The Detroit Public School system in the first two-thirds of the Twentieth Century had an extraordinary music program, with many schools' music programs led by classically-trained German-born teachers. A local piano company, Grinnell's, ensured that any household that wanted a piano would get one, at whatever tiny monthly payment could be made. Indeed, Detroit could not have become the Arsenal of Democracy, nor would it have been the richest city in the United States in the 1950's, had the productive powers of labor not been nourished by the beauty of western Classical culture. (That is a story for another time.)

The tragedy for Detroit and for the nation is that the very principles upon which such progress and happiness were based, were not understood. Thus, when those principles came under attack by the financial predators of the British empire and their counter-cultural warriors, they were nearly destroyed. In her Zhuhai speech, Helga Zepp-LaRouche said, "In all great cultures there have been thinkers who understood the deep connections between an optimistic image of the limitless moral and intellectual self-perfectibility of man, with the pursuit of the common good as the precondition for the long-term survival of society, and the cohesion between human creativity and the laws of the physical universe." That knowledge must be the basis for freeing the minds of the American people.

November 2, 1988

Beethoven as a Physical Scientist

by Lyndon H. LaRouche, Jr.

Preface to the first publication, in the* EIR *of May 26, 1989

Executive Intelligence Review *is pleased to publish in a preliminary version the following paper, originally written by Lyndon LaRouche on Nov. 2, 1988. We believe that the ideas here are so crucial to the survival of our civilization, that there should be no further delay in making them widely available. Not all of the illustrations originally called for by Mr. LaRouche have been sufficiently researched to be publishable at this time, and this is partly due to the fact of the author's trial and unjust imprisonment as of Jan. 27, 1989, which has made it difficult for him to personally guide the scientific work at the necessary pace.—The Editors.*

EIRNS/Stuart Lewis

The author gives a class in geometry and physical economy in 1985, at the barn of Ibykus Farm in Loudoun County, Virginia.

Like a skilled cabaret mimic, purporting to mimic well-known public figures of politics and entertainment, significant numbers of professional musicians have produced short improvisations which audiences might recognize as parodies of a Mozart, Beethoven, Schubert, and so forth. Yet none of them could have produced a composition which might be confused with an actual work of those or other classical composers.

Thus, the ability to compose artistic statements in the literate language of music common to all classical composers, is virtually as lost today as the ancient Egyptian was lost until the discovery of the Rosetta Stone. Fortunately, the almost language of classical composition can be reconstructed, and the result proven conclusively to be an accurate one. This accomplishment is one of the leading projects which this aging writer is determined to see completed before he "shuffles off this mortal coil."

It is the solution to that problem, which is identified here.

The timing of the appearance of this report reflects the recent progress of work on the subject of Eugenio Beltrami's crucial discoveries respecting the negative curvature of physical space-time. Crucial proof of Beltrami's corrective supplement to Riemann curvature renders intelligible to a much deeper degree, the otherwise empirically demonstrable principles of composition of classical music. It is therefore the appropriate time to publish a summary account of key points of progress toward the goal of defining rigorously the principles employed by such composers as Bach, Mozart, and Beethoven.

Excepting the indispensable function of advanced geometries, for rendering musical principles truly intelligible, most of the pieces of evidence to be brought together are already well-known among relevant classes of scholars and fine-aaarts professionals.

The principle of natural beauty, for example, has remained constant in classical fine arts, including music, since before the time of Plato in ancient Greece. It is also more or less well-known among relevant scholars and professionals, that the mere imitation of natural beauty, as we find it common to the morphology of growth and function of living processes, is not sufficient to class a painting or song as a work of classical fine art. While remaining ever-faithful to demonstrable harmonic principles of natural beauty, the work of art must incorporate and radiate that special quality of mental life which sets mankind apart from, and above the beasts: the unique potential of persons, the development of the creative powers of the human mind.

Respecting classical musical composition as such, most of what is verified as knowledge of the performing techniques of the eighteenth and early nineteenth centuries, is either valid beyond doubt, or, at worst, not untruthful as far as it goes. The breakdown in knowledge occurs wherever modern professional musicology, as taught in the relevant classrooms of universities and music conservatories, is confronted with a topic which bears upon presenting the method of composition commonly employed by classical composers in the form of an intelligible, and verifiable principle.

The most immediate, practical objective of this undertaking, is both to enhance the powers of the best classical performers, and to enable amateurs among their audiences to read a classical score as the composer intended it should be read. More broadly, the purpose is to develop means by aid of which the beauties of the greatest classical fine arts might more easily beautify and otherwise enrich spiritually the lives of the vast numbers of persons suffering the frightening pangs of spiritual want, experienced by all who lack enrichment of this aspect of their living.

Had a student of music been reared in the relevant places in western Europe, during the period from Brunelleschi's Florence, through as late as 1849, he or she would have learned to speak the language of classical musical composition in a literate degree, and with comprehension of principles involved as intelligible ones. Since the language of classical poetry and music has been lost, in that sense, over a period of more than a hundred years, to adduce the same principles of literacy today is far more difficult than would have been the case in those earlier times.

For reasons to be indicated here, the required reconstruction can not be accomplished without reference to principles of physics associated with the work of such as Gauss, Riemann, Beltrami, and Georg Cantor, during the mid-portion of the nineteenth century. It is certain that Ludwig van Beethoven did not know his principles in that form of representation; yet, in a relevant sense, he mastered those principles very well, as we, today, can show beyond all reasonable doubt.

Hence, it is not only permissible to refer to Beethoven as a physical scientist; under today's circumstances, it is more or less mandatory that we do so.

On this account, the author has adopted the view, that no statement of principles of composition is truly intelligible and also verifiable musically, unless it enables professional musicians to reach a point of breakthrough to deeper understanding of the most astonishing episode in all classical composition, the exemplary compositions of Beethoven's last period of work. The last quartets, including the "Great Fugue," beginning with Opus 127, should be singled out as the most concentrated expression of this most challenging episode in the entire history of music to date.

The proof that any progress in unravelling this singular episode is valid, depends upon showing that Beethoven's principles during that last period of his work are coherent with what we may adduce from study of the most relevant work of J. S. Bach. For musical-historical reasons, the simplest way to establish that connection is the influence of Bach's "Musical Offering" on the leading work of Mozart, Beethoven, Schubert, and Chopin, for example, later. (**Figure 1.**)

A re-examination of the work called "Bach's Art of the Fugue," must be considered from the standpoint of what the later work of Beethoven shows to be the deeper principles embedded implicitly in the Bach canons of polyphony, as later composer's treatment of the "Musical Offering" enables us to trace the connections most explicitly.

ASCENDING

J.S. Bach, *Musical Offering,* Ricercar à 3 voci

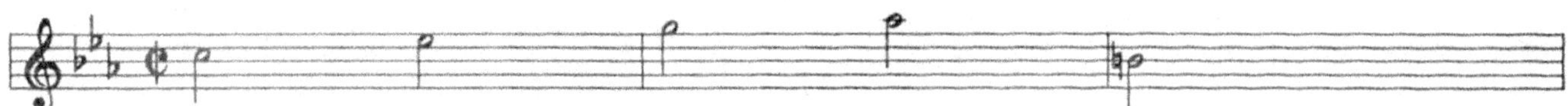

W.A. Mozart, Sonata for Piano in C minor, K. 457

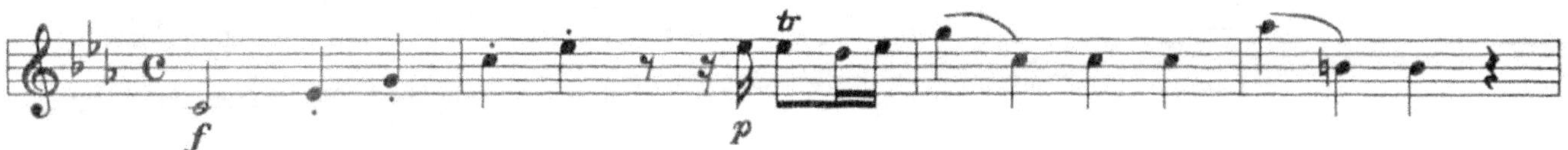

W. A. Mozart, Quartet for 2 Violins, Viola, and Violoncello, K. 465 ("Dissonant")

The Singing of Classical Poetry

In physical science, except as we demonstrate the power to create physical states which have not existed in the known universe before man's artificing such states, every valid fundamental discovery in physics is premised upon what are termed "crucial experiments" showing a fallacy in reading of what nature has already accomplished. Such is the history of music.

With aid of development of what is known as the study of non-linear spectroscopy of optical biophysical processes, we are enabled to understand, as a matter of biological princ- iple, whence certain characteristic and crucial features of the singing and hearing of a sung bel-canto scale pivotted on either Middle C at 256 cycles, or approximately midway between 256 and 257, a value almost precisely 42 octaves below the characteristic frequency of living DNA. (**Table 1.**)

However, earlier, excepting the influence of the physics work summed up by Johannes Kepler, the development of classical principles of singing and musical polyphony generally was premised upon the empirics of what we reference today as the "bel canto" trained singing voice.

The classical, man-made musical instruments were designed on the basis of physical principles adduced from empirics of the "bel canto" form of singing voice, and were constructed in conformity with the assumption of the value of Middle C as exactly, or nearly C=256. The different species of stringed instruments and wind instruments were treated as an extension of the polyphonic choir composed of various species of singing voices, and the principles of vocal polyphony were imposed upon the instrumental voices, to the effect that the very notion of an "instrumental interpretation," differing from a vocal one, is a bestializing absurdity contrary to the most elementary principle of classical composition.

The root of music is the singing of classical poetry. The polyphonic singing of classical poetry is uniquely the origin of the tonal construction of the well-tempered musical scale, and of the metrical structure of musical composition. (The attribution of the metrical structure of music to an origin in the dance, as that hoaxster Richard Wagner insisted, is based upon Nietzschean aesthetics, as the Romantic and Modernist dogmas trace the origins of music to the eroticism of the phrygian cult of Nietzsche's Satan-Dionysos.)

As early as Vedic hymns located by included solar-astronomical evidence to no later than 4,000 B.C., any classical poem is also a musical score. The physical

DESCENDING

J.S. Bach, *Musical Offering*, Ricercar à 3 voci

W. A. Mozart, Sonata for Piano in C minor, K. 457

W. A. Mozart, Quartet for 2 Violins, Viola, and Violoncello, K. 465 ("Dissonant")

basis for this well-known and practiced fact, in the singing of classical poetry, was first explored rigorously by Leonardo da Vinci, who was first to document the changes in pitch inherent in shifting enunciation from one vowel, or consonant-inflected vowel, to another. [**Table 2** illustrates this point for the vowels alone, without consonant inflection, in a first approximation. **Figure 2** is a table of vowels in combination with various consonants prepared by Leonardo da Vinci.]

For example, during the course of the nineteenth century, in Germany, these studies by Leonardo were combined with bel-canto principles of voice production, to provide the program for training of both singers and classical dramatic actors.

The differences in intonation of the vowels, as each literate form of language defines the intonation somewhat differently, does not define an absolute, fixed tone, for that vowel, or consonant-inflected vowel. What is fixed is the relative value of the intervals separating these intonations from one another.

In both classical poetry, and classical song based upon classical poetry, the absolute value of the intonation of a vowel or consonant-inflected vowel shifts as the reference tone for C set to, for example, Guido's "ut" [see Table 2, Guidonian singing scale] changes. This is easily demonstrated by reference to the practice of placing a sequence of tones in the bass part, as pedal-point, and using those tones as the reference tones for the choices of absolute tone-values corresponding to the selected intervals among the indication vowels and consonant-inflected vowels.

Thus, the prosodic determination of the intervals now interacts, in both classical reciting of poetry, and classical song, with an harmonically ordered sequence of tones in the actual or implicit pedal-point. These pedal-point sequences are either directly the Kepler intervals, or consistent derivatives of those intervals, such as the well-tempered octave-scale itself: octave, fifth, fourth, major third, minor third. In constructive geometry, this interaction is represented as doubly-connected action.

However, actual musical composition must reference immediately two additional degrees of such interaction, confronting us with an elementary musical domain which is, respectively, triply-connected, and quadruply-connected.

From the human singing voice, we have the following consideration. Each species of singing voice is characterized, in each of all cases, by a set of unique

Ascending and Descending Sequences in Nine Related Musical Compositions

ASCENDING

W. A. Mozart, Fantasy K. 475

L. v. Beethoven, Sonata for Piano in C minor, Op. 13 ("Pathétique")

L. v. Beethoven, Sonata in C minor for Violin and Piano, Op. 30, No. 2

L. v. Beethoven, Sonata for Piano in C minor, Op. 111

F. Chopin, Sonata for Piano in C minor, Op. 4

F. Schubert, Sonata for Piano in C minor, D. 958 (Posthumous)

DESCENDING

W. A. Mozart, Fantasy, K. 475

L. v. Beethoven, Sonata for Piano in C minor, Op. 13 ("Pathétique")

L. v. Beethoven, Sonata for Piano and Violin in C minor, Op. 30, No. 2

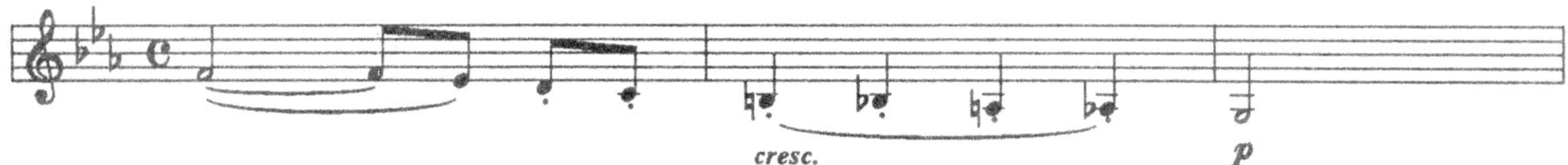

L. v. Beethoven, Sonata for Piano in C minor, Op. 111

F. Chopin, Sonata for Piano in C minor, Op. 4

F. Schubert, Sonata for Piano in C minor, D. 958 (Posthumous)

intervals of the well-tempered scale, referenced to C=256, at which the quality of the singing voice must change (or incur damage to the singing voice). (See **Figure 3**).

So, when the classical composer sets a classical poem to song, the composer must chose, in the simplest case, a definite species of male or female singing voice. He must choose a major or minor key-signature, such as C-major or C-minor, which causes the natural voice-register shift of the bel-canto-trained singer to change quality at some desired place in the vocal line.

Thus, as the table shows, a song written for a species of female voice might be transposed for another female voice, but not for a species of male voice, without losing something important in the classical composer's original musical intent. The distribution of register-shift intervals in the male voices differ from the distribution in the female voices.

In the case of vocal polyphony, using perhaps two different species of female voices (e.g., soprano and mezzo-soprano, or tenor and bass or baritone), the classical composer is confronted with some interesting problems, on account of the principle just referenced. The simplest canon, based on such a polyphonic combination of species of voices, incurs extremely fascinating requirements.

The intent of the poem as a poem, as read by the composer, must be served. Hence, the natural voice-register shifts of all of the voices must be treated accordingly.

This fascinating problem in the most elementary feature of the composition of the classical principles of polyphony, even in the form of the simplest canonical exercises, defines the most rudimentary features of the principles of well-tempered counterpoint.

These voice-registration considerations must be superimposed upon the doubly-connected domain identified above. In the language of constructive geometry, the most rudimentary classical counterpoint is already triply-connected.

In the cases of the instruments, we must expand the notion of counterpoint, without changing any underlying principle. We must treat each instrument as a species of singing voice, and view its intrinsic registral characteristics accordingly. The case of the duet between a classical soprano oboe, constructed with reference to C=256, and a true soprano or mezzo-soprano, is among the most beautiful phenomena in the repertoire, and thus beautifully instructive of the point we have just made. The same relationships, with differences duly noted, are relevant to all cases.

Yet, except as such triple-connectedness is applied to the interpretation of classical poetry for composition of song, we have not exceeded the domain of natural beauty. In all cases of exercizes in classical counterpoint according to the principles of triple-connectedness, we have not yet bridged the distinction between the imitation of natural beauty and fine art.

TABLE 1
The Musical Scale and the Biological Spectra

Mitogenic radiation	42 octaves + F-341 Hz (200 nanometers)
Pure protein alpha helix	42 octaves + E-326 Hz (208 nanometers)
DNA	42 octaves + C-256 Hz (265 nanometers)
Protein complex	42 octaves + B-243 Hz (280 nanometers)
Vision (lower bound)	42 octaves + G-188 Hz (360 nanometers)

Register shift between ultraviolet and visible F—F-sharp

Chlorophyll-*a*	42 octaves + E-158 Hz (430 nanometers)
Carotene	42 octaves + D-141.5 Hz (481 nanometers)
Photosynthesis action spectra	42 octaves + C-128 Hz (536 nanometers)
Vision peak	42 octaves + B-122 Hz (560 nanometers)
Cytochrome	42 octaves + B-flat-114Hz (595 nanometers)
Chlorophyll-*a*	42octaves + A-flat-102.25Hz (660 nanometers)
Bacteria photosynthesis center 1	42 octaves + G-94 Hz (720 nanometers)

Register shift between visible and infrared F—F-sharp

Bacteria photosynthesis center 2	42 octaves + E-80 Hz (850 nanometers)
Bacteria photosynthesis center 3	42 octaves + E-flat 75.5 Hz (900 nanometers)
Biosphere maximum radiation	42 octaves + C-64 (1,072 nanometers)

The key moments of biological processes range 42 octaves up from the F above middle C to the C two octaves below middle C, which is itself 40 octaves above C =256. All values are precise musical tones in cycles per second (Hz) plus 42 octaves. The initial experimental values in wavelengths are given in parentheses.

Source: Warren J. Hamerman, "The Musicality of Living Processes," *21st Century Science & Technology*, March-April, 1 989, p. 34. Reprinted by permission.

In true classical fine art, whether in painting, architecture, city-planning, drama, poetry, or music, we must never violate adducible lawful principles of natural beauty in the composition as a unit-conception; yet, unless this is accomplished by adding something crucial, it is mere describing of nature, and, however useful that description might be, it is not yet a creative work, and hence not a work of classical fine art.

The essence of music, which carries it beyond a mere description of natural beauty, is the use of the medium of natural beauty as the medium of expression of the creative powers of the individual human mind. These are the same powers represented by the generation of a valid fundamental discovery in physical science.

Most briefly, merely to identify the point: The characteristic of classical music, is the lawful generation of a combination of harmonic and metrical dissonances, typified in harmonics by the interval between C nd F♯.

TABLE 2
Vowel harmony: relative pitch of Italian vowels
(based upon second formant, F²)

A) Transposed down one octave

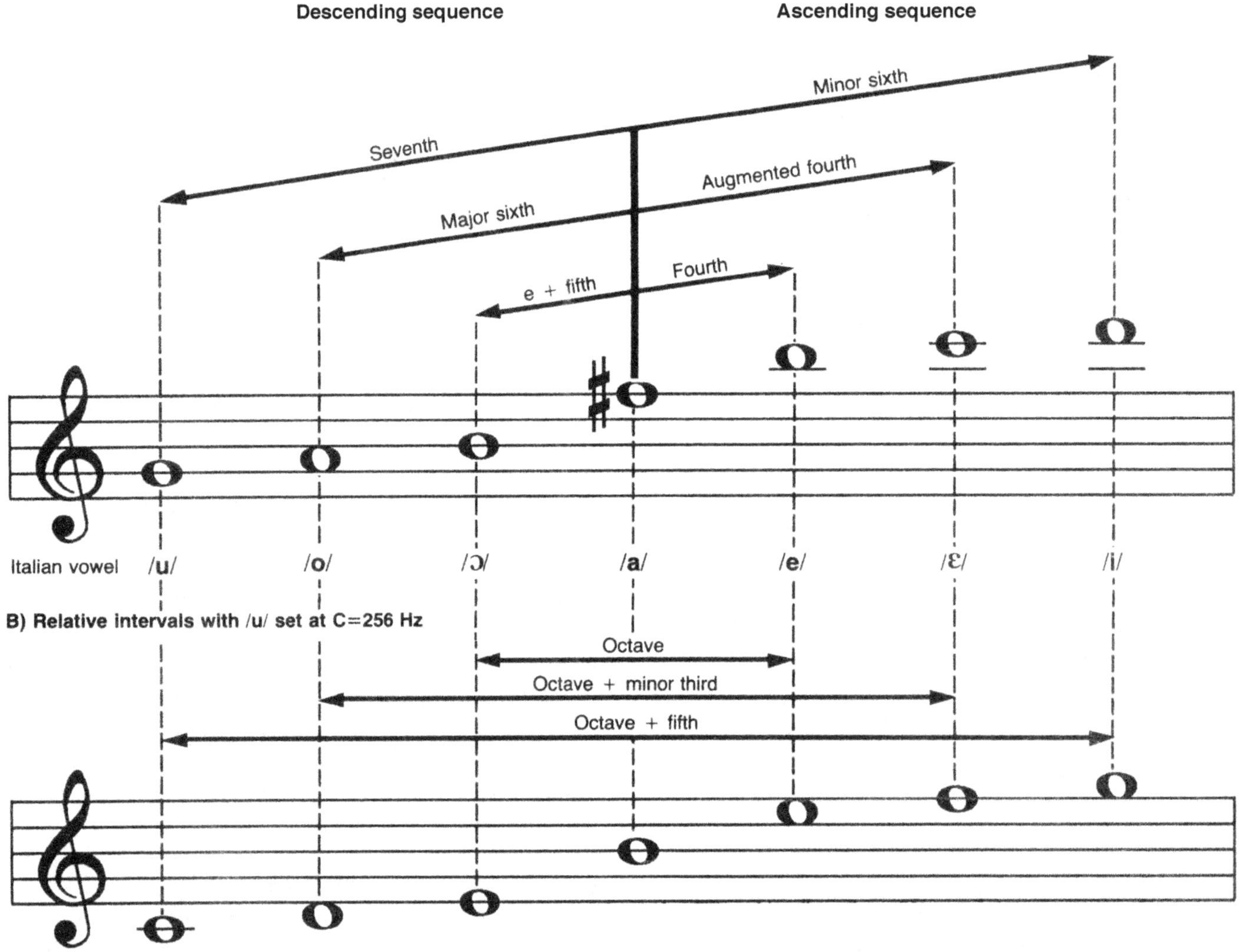

The musical quality of vowels in speech is lawfully determined. This chart shows the musical-interval relations among the seven Italian vowels based upon vowel quality. It is based upon recent studies of native Italian speakers and is derived from the second formant, or resonance peak, as measured for the different vowels in Hertz. The test data was based upon men's voices only. For clarity, the tones have been transposed down one octave in (A). In (B) the intervals have been transposed so that the /u/ vowel corresponds to the syllable "ut" (the first tone of the Guidonian singing scale) set at middle C of 256 Hertz.

Leonardo da Vinci's Chart of Vowels

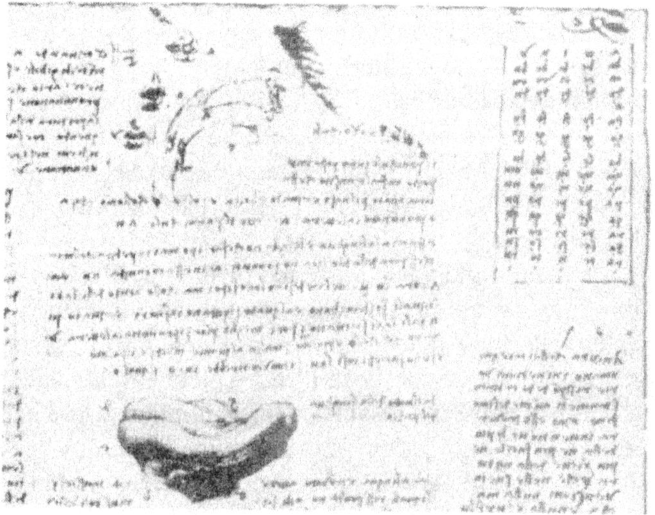

Leonardo showed his interest in the apparatus of voice production in this sheet of studies which includes a detailed analysis of the tongue muscles, and a chart of vowels combined with various consonants (upper right corner).

F♯ is the tone at which the soprano voice must shift naturally to a higher register, and the tenor must pass from the second to third register, so. Thus, the soprano and tenor voices divide the octave referenced to C=256 into two tetrachords, as a study of the score of the relevant *urtext* of songs of Mozart, Beethoven. and Schubert illustrate the point.

The *relative* dissonance must never be reached arbitrarily, as irrationalist forms of composition, such as chromatic Romanticism, Modernism, and jazz do. It must never occur except as a necessary occurrence within the elaboration of polyphony according to lawful principles of classical counterpoint.

The essential feature of any classical composition as a work of art is the generation and resolution of such combined harmonic and metrical *relative* dissonances. Having posed the occurrence of such *relative* dissonances as a musical problem, the composer must resolve that problem. The composer must elaborate a process of contrapuntal development, as Beethoven does with his musical-compositional montages, which carries the process of composition as a whole to a resolution. At the end, the affirmation of the resolution imparts to the listener's mind the fact that a complete musical idea has been stated. At least, this is the case if the performance of the entire composition has been articulated to effect a kind of "long phrasing" which is coextensive with the performance as an entirety.

This problem and its resolution, completed by the final sequence of tones of concluding affirmation, represents a musical idea. Nothing less does.

Among the best available, simpler illustrations of this process, is the surviving notes of Beethoven bearing upon the compositional pre-history of his Opus 106 "Hammerklavier" piano sonata. The fact on which we wish the reader to focus, is the enormous span of intellectual work which occupied Beethoven in successive revisions of the design of what became the opening thematic statement of that composition.

In effect, in this work, Beethoven was working backwards, from the definition of a musical idea, to shaping a germinal thematic statement, whose contrapuntal elaboration would lead to the generation of the musical idea through such a compositional process.

Later, in referencing the last stages of polishing of the completed composition, and in viewing the succeeding piano sonatas, Opus 109, 110, and 111, as a unit of compositional process output, we see Beethoven's repeated retrospective reference to the same musical idea which preoccupied Mozart before him, that of J. S. Bach's "Musical Offering."

By considering the Opus 106 in these enlarged terms of reference, we see more deeply. Note the prefixed amendment of the second movement of the 106, the *Adagio Sostenuto*. Note the last movement, its great double fugue. Compare the conclusion of these series of compositions, the Opus 111, with the first movement, and more, of Chopin's "funeral march" sonata.

It ought to be obvious that Beethoven's last quartets, beginning with the Opus 127, and including the Great Fugue Opus 133, must be treated as a unit-series of exposition of the same species of musical idea, in the same sense that the Opus 106, 109, 110, 111, must be viewed as a unit-idea series.

This sequence of unit-idea series, in Beethoven's last period of composition, beg comparison with a succession of stages of valid scientific revolutions. Each unit-series of compositions is much more than a specific musical composition; it is a musical scientific revolution, from which music must not turn backwards. Hence, the occurrence of these so emphatically in clusters of closely related compositions, even much more so than in Beethoven's earlier publishing practice.

In the simplest of all possible cases, an harmonic series corresponding to a creative developmental process may be referenced to no less than three notes, and the same interval expressed by other sequences of notes. On this account, and expanded considerations, the minimal requirement of any classical musical composition is that it be defined as a quadruply-connected process of composition.

We mean that statement in the fullest sense of the topological implications of a such a statement. This brings our inquiry, implicitly, into the mathematical-physics domain of Gauss, Dirichlet, Weierstrass, Riemann, Cantor, and the great Beltrami.

Science and Music Are 'Non-Euclidean'

For this writer, any effort dedicated to the defense and enrichment of the practice of classical fine arts, classical music most emphatically, is always a labor of love. That is the principal motivating purpose here; however, this report and the shaping of its content as a whole, are prompted by three additional considerations.

1) Modern Western European civilization, including that of North and South America equally, rests upon the reaffirmation and further development of Augustinian principles accomplished by chiefly the fifteenth-century Italian Renaissance, as centered around the work of the 1439 Council of Florence. Modern classical fine art is an integral part of the continued functioning of that heritage.

Presently, the very existence of that civilization is imperilled by cultural warfare against everything associated with the Augustinian heritage generally, and the heritage of the Council of Florence most emphatically. The most visible expression of this cultural warfare imperilling our civilization is everything typified by bolshevism and the satanic influences centered around the

---

FIGURE 3
The Six Species of the Human Singing-Voice

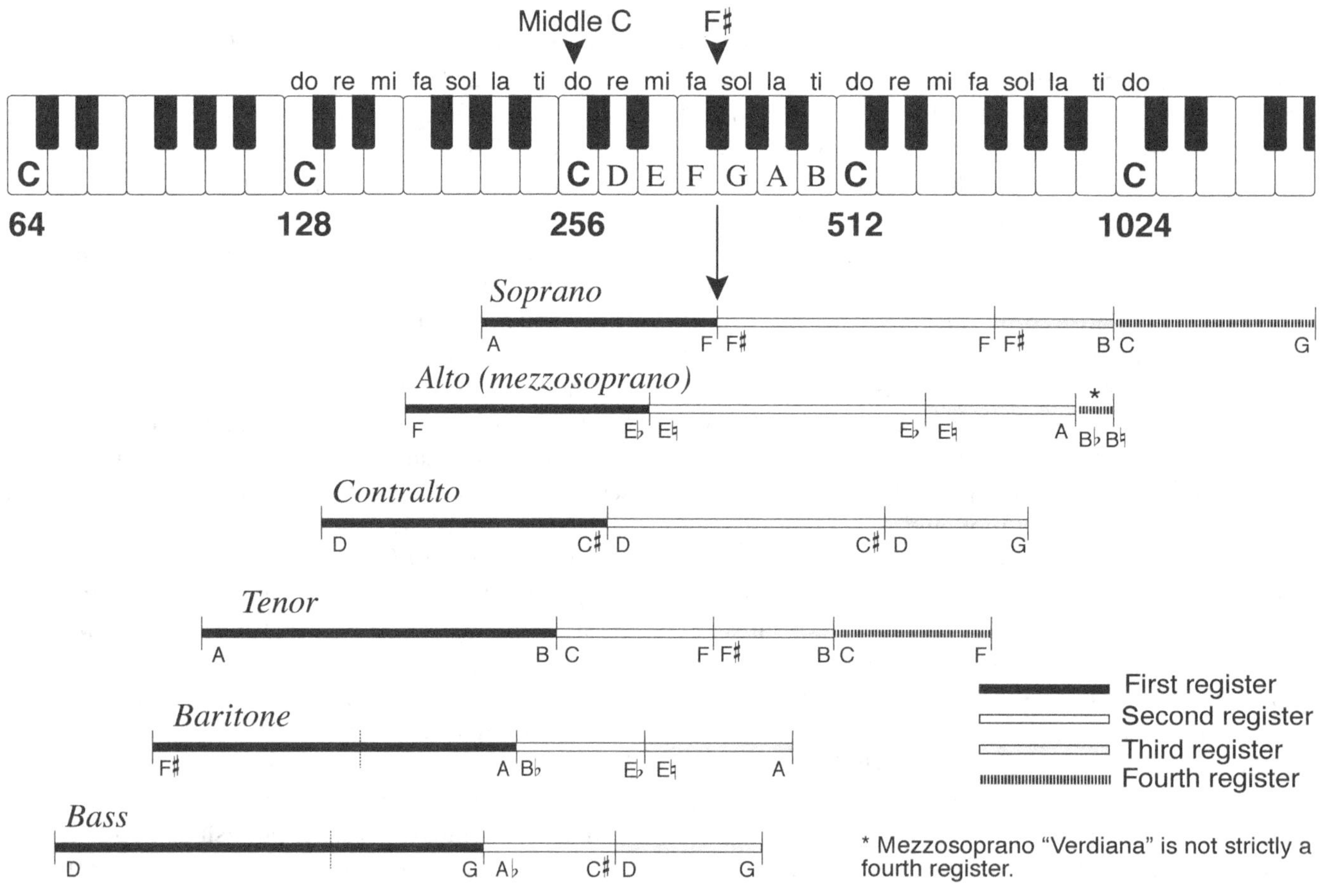

Source: Schiller Institute research team. Ranges are based on known examples in the classical vocal repertoire.

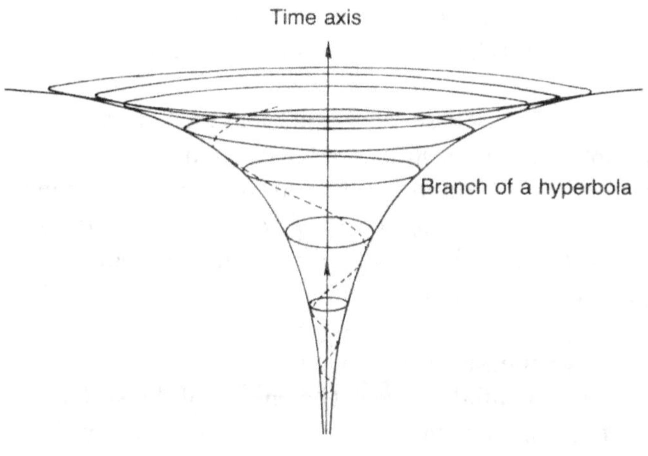

The surface of revolution of one branch of the hyperbola is the least-action representation of the process of the flaring horn. This mapping of the singularities of a Riemannian hyperspherical continuum is correct, but ultimately inadequate.

work of Theodore Adorno's Frankfurt School, and the satanic evil of the Adorno-Arendt dogma of "the authoritarian personality," the cultural dogma of the modern Anti-Christ.

Under such circumstances, the defense of classical music against both the Muscovite influence and the quite literally satanic irrationalism of such as Adorno, is an indispensable feature of the defense of Western civilization as a whole.

This defense requires that principles of music be liberated from the authority of sundry musicological and related cults of "art for art's sake," including the gifted Shenker's false, Helmholtzian dogmas on tuning and irrationalist absurdity of "absolute music." The essence of classical fine art is, as we have indicated for classical music, not a matter of varying mere musicological opinions; classical composition expresses a principle which is implicitly a fully intelligible one, and subject to the same authority of proof as a theorem in physics.

2) The intelligible representation of a quadruply-connected manifold, the minimal conception of classical composition, is, at a minimum a proposition in topology lying specifically within the domain of Riemannian physics. However, this representation is not, by itself, an adequate one.

The functional mapping of the singularities of a Ri-emannian hyperspherical continuum, is merely approximated by the relevant point-set mapping of hyperbolic-trigonometric forms of discontinuities. That mapping is correct, as far as it goes, but is ultimately an inadequate one. (Cf. Figure 4—model of an ordinary hyperbola.)

In brief, on this specific point, self-evident points do not exist in the non-euclidean constructive geometry upon which the Gauss-Riemann complex domain rests. Therefore, the existence of such determined points, as points, has no causal significance in a continuing, non-linear process, but the purely negative one, discontinuity, addressed by Dirichlet. Had the Riemann Surface Function been examined more thoroughly than it has been, this problematic feature of that function would have received wider attention than it enjoyed in the hands of Riemann's student, collaborator and critic, Eugenio Beltrami.

This problem has systematic relevance for thorough comprehension of the quadruply-connected, minimal domain of classical musical composition. It has crucial relevance for leading questions of experimental physics today.

The problem is, to restate the nature of the Riemannian point-set, both with respect to each point and to the topology of the Riemann Surface as a whole, to the effect of eliminating the paradoxical nature of the point as such. The solution of that paradox accords, at first and second impressions, with Beltrami's arguments on the subject of negative curvature. Beltrami's argument accords also with the writer's geometrical definition of *negentropy*, as adduced from a refutation of a related problem, his refutation of the axiomatic fallacy underlying the so-called Kantian Paradox. This bears also upon the solution to the Parmenides Paradox, whose form of solution is the central feature of Nicolaus of Cusa's work founding modern non-euclidean geometry, *De Docta Ignorantia* [*On Learned Ignorance*]. The writer's own formal solution to the Parmenides Paradox was elaborated as a feature of his refutation of Kant.

The writer has identified some of a set of crucial experimental problems of present-day physics, which beg implicitly the issues of Beltramian negative curvature, and has proposed that the history of the development of the conceptual basis of modern physics be traced from relevant work of Brunelleschi, to the present, to the purpose of putting the conceptual nature of the problems in appropriate historical focus.

The history of the refinement of the principles of classical polyphony, since the period of Brunelleschi, through the work of Kepler and beyond, is interwined with the developments leading into the articulation of Beltramian negative curvature. Otherwise as indicated proximately above, there are conceptions bearing upon the principles of classical composition which beg attention to the same conceptual matters.

3) The memoranda which this writer has circulated earlier to sundry scientists and other researchers, on the subject of an historical background approach to the issues of beltramian negative curvature, have already borne useful fruit, including a report on relevant work-to-date among the writer's associates, including a significant such report by Dino de Paoli.

Elements of that latter report help to situate the issues of quadruple-connectedness. I shall quote passages from that report, and reference some of the illustrations supplied.

A surface of constant negative curvature, or the so-called Beltrami pseudosphere, has the topological characteristic of triple connectivity. There are at least two singularities built into the surface, which does not allow a simple topological closure. In contrast, a surface of constant positive curvature, or the so-called Riemannian sphere, has the topology of a simply connected surface, with only two poles instead of singularities. (See **Figure 5.**)

Beltrami himself could not find a full physical meaning for such a surface, except the obvious one of a surface of minimum action.

The direction you indicate seems to me absolutely the right one. I had an unfinished idea on the use of the Beltrami Surface as representing a potential surface characterizing what are indicated today as *gravitational* and *strong* (nuclear) interaction, for reasons I have to elaborate fully.

The positively curved surface, represents the potential surface of the so-called *weak* and *electromagnetic* interaction, which it is known are coupled. The unification of all interactions in the direction of a *continuous* surface, where the positive/negative curvatures are not simple polars, but where indeed the negative represents "holes," but of the Beltrami type.

"The dissymmetry in the negative/postive

ratio allows the definition of absolute time, and the consequent non-respect [non-correspondence] of the conservation of energy in a single manifold (the neutrino problem, for example).

He then discusses some simpler kinds of crucial-experimental demonstrations. He turns first to the geometry of the generation of the shock-wave, in Riemann's 1859 *On The Propagation of Plane Air Waves of Finite Magnitude*. Referencing an example developed in his published article on Leonardo da Vinci,

Take the surface of water as representing an equipotential surface. The energy of the surface tension is then seen geometrically. A simple sine-wave, including a soliton, is characterized and mathematically representable by a surface of positive curvature (elliptic function). (See **Figure 6.**)

The formation of water breakers—that is, the "breaking of the surface"—creates a topological transformation, given that the breaks, or holes, or singularities increase the connectivity, and, mathematically, with shift to hyperbolic functions (Beltrami). That is, a surface of negative curvature. This is the shock-wave description [of this phenomenon, according to the referenced paper of Riemann].

Referencing his papers published earlier, he supplies a second simple kind of crucial illustration. His reference to the glass of wine should signify a wine-glass whose bowl is of constant positive curvature, and red wine produces the clearest results for laymen repeating this demonstration.

If you take a glass of wine, and put it in front of a lamp, the projection of light on the table does not produce a *point-light*, but a characteristic figure called a *caustic*. (**Figure 7.**)

If you try to transform persective linearly on a curved surface, a simplistic interpretation of the so-called *Leonardo* curved perspective, you end up with the following problem. Your *focal points* are no longer points, but *caustics*. (**Figure 8.**)

He concludes with the following summary:

A) Surfaces of constant negative curvature elaborated by Beltrami

A-1 Solid generated by the rotation of a caustic

A-2 Pseudosphere generated by a tractrix (see Figure 5C)

A-3 Catenoid type generated by rotation of a catenary or a cycloid (see Figure 5C)

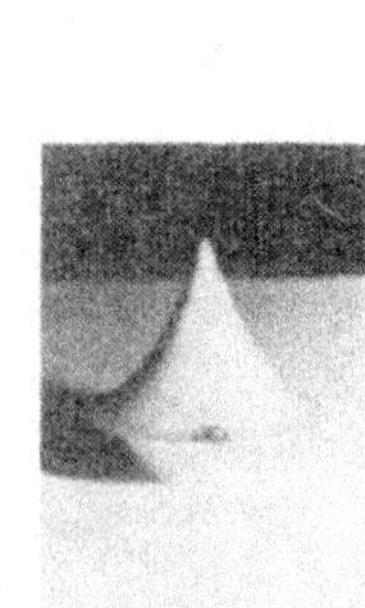
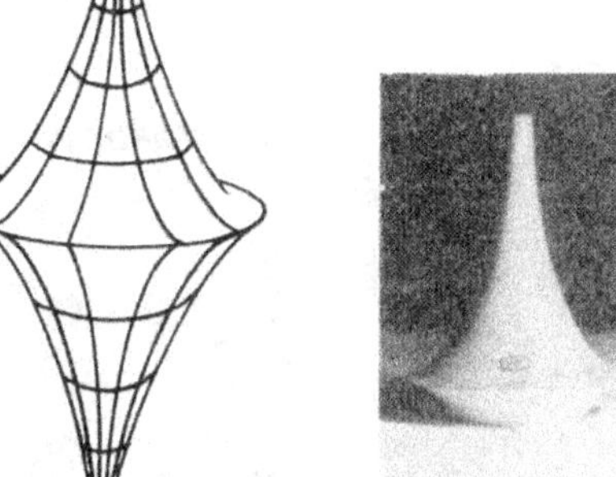
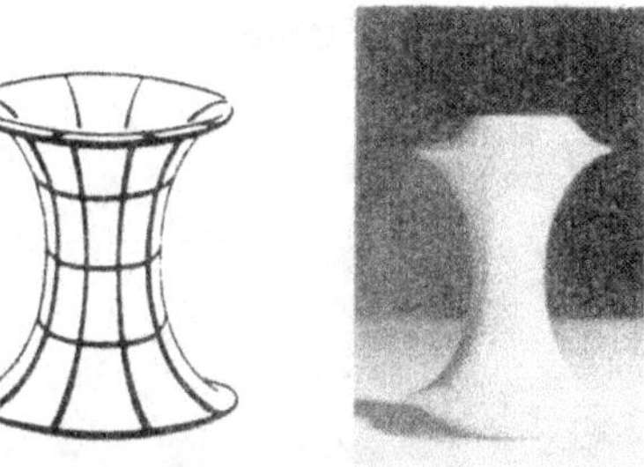

Beltrami showed that there are only three constructible solids of constant negative curvature. He named only one of these, the pseudosphere. The photos by Dino de Paoli show Eugenio Beltrami's original models, which are kept at the University of Pavia in Italy.

B) Multiply connected surfaces

Sphere

Torus

Pretzel

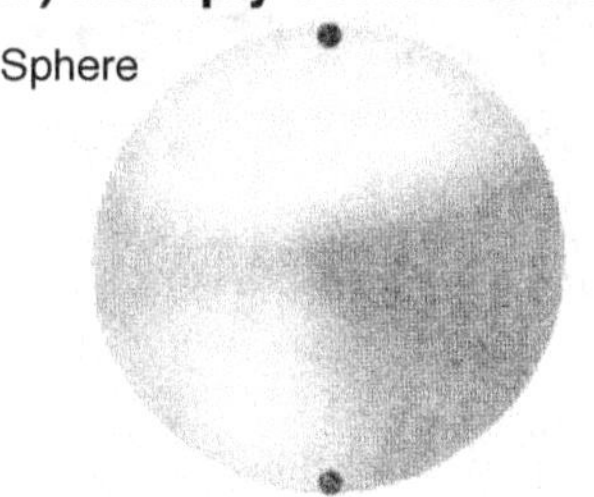

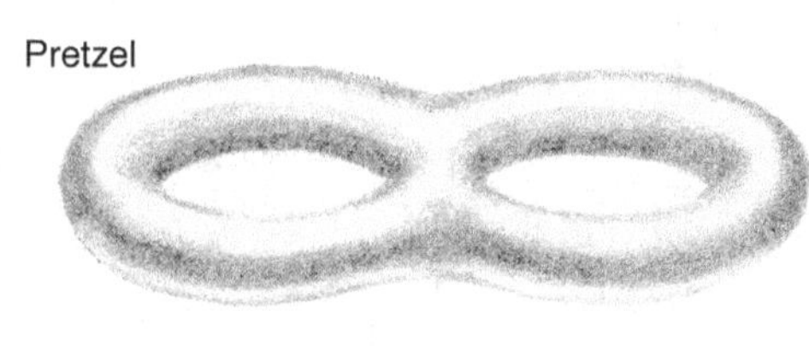

The topology of the projection of a sphere (constant positive curvature) has simple connectivity; there are no singularities (holes), only poles. The projection of a torus, with its center hole, is doubly connected, and the projection of a pretzel shape, with two holes, is triply connected.

C) The catenary and the tractrix
C-1 **C-2**

D) Combination of two negative surfaces generated by the catenary and tractrix

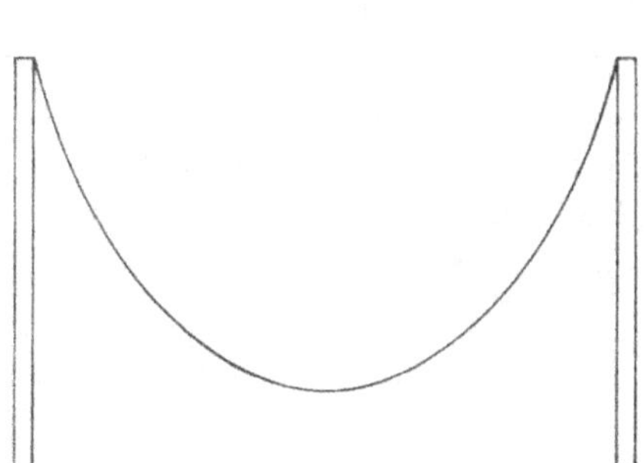
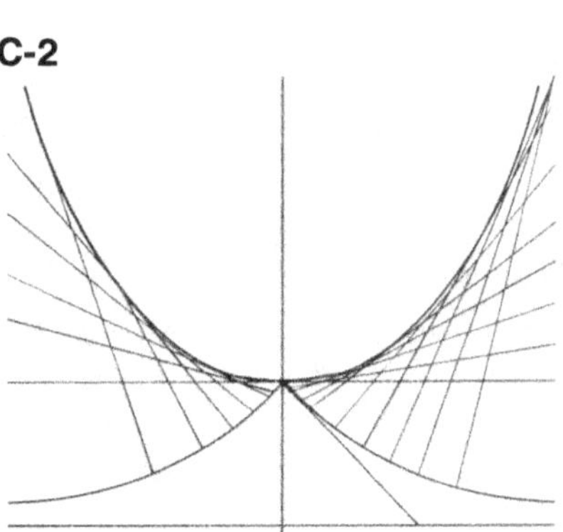
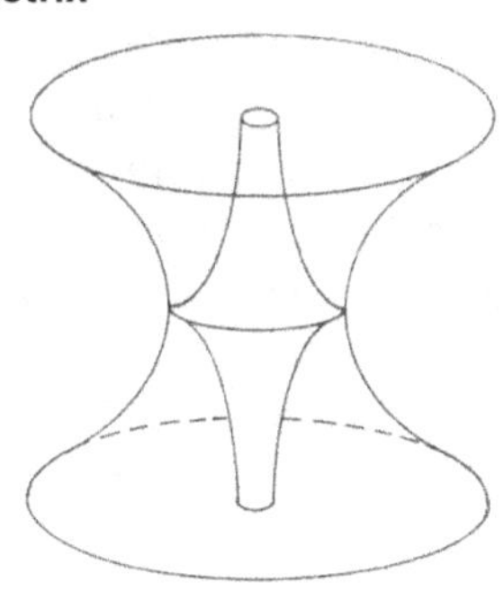

The catenary is the form assumed by a chain or rope suspended from two fixed points and hanging under its own weight (C-1). To find the involute of a catenary (or of any curve), imagine a thread on the surface of the curve, which is then cut and unwound from the lowest point on the curve to the left and right. The ends of the thread on a catenary rope trace out the tractrix shown below. Each step of the unwinding is like constructing a tangent of the catenary to the tractrix. If the normal (perpendicular) is drawn to the tangent of the tractrix at any point, it can be seen that this normal becomes a tangent to the catenary. Note that all tangents from the inside of the tractrix to its base are equal in length.

Of this type of curve, called "mechanical curve," the most general is the cycloid. The cycloid is important in two respects: It has the physical characteristic of being the path which requires the least time for a body to descend from one point to another (brachistochrone). Also, descending bodies all arrive at the end of the curve at the same time, independently of the initial position (isochrone).

A) Simple Sine-Wave with Underlying Parabolic Geometry

B) Formation of a Breaker: Schematic

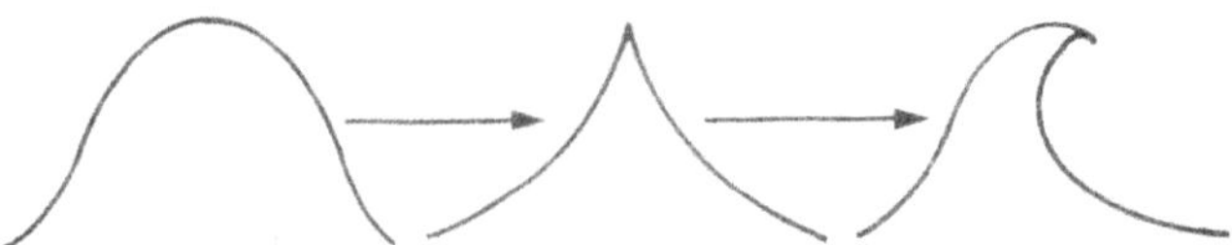

C) Leonardo's drawing of wave with breakers forming

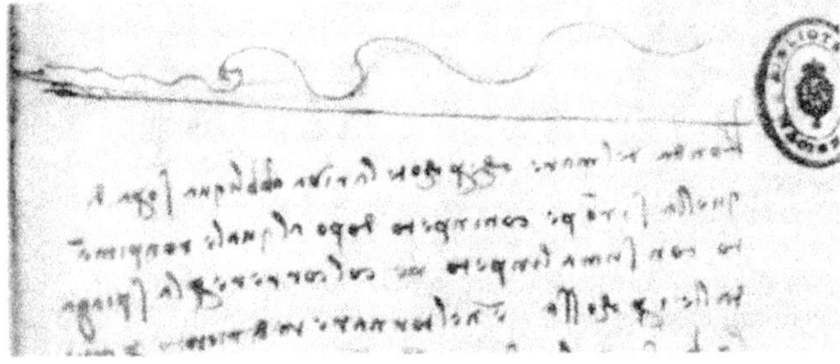

D) Breaker with surf-rider

E) Theory of characteristics

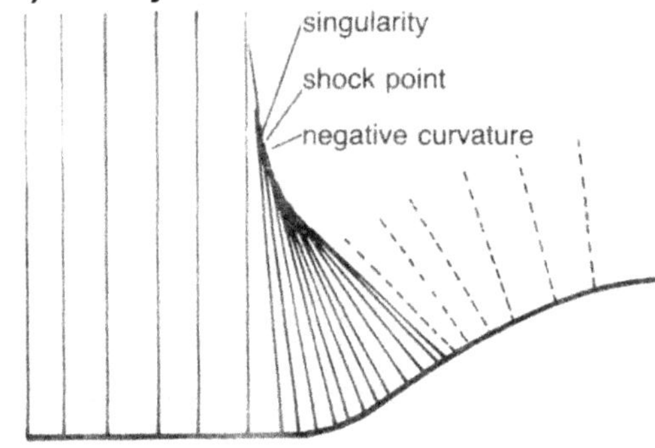

What Riemann called "geometric characteristics" and Leonardo called "cross waves," are represented by perpendicular lines when the speed is constant, and bend right or left when the speed increases or decreases, for example due to enlarging or narrowing the passage through which a fluid is flowing. Thus it will appear that the characteristics touch. Riemann used this to represent a shock wave. It is also a singularity. It is also, clearly, negative curvature, which therefore appears in connection with the formation of a singularity.

The amount of Leonardo's illustration on this field, and on the related reflection on a curved surface, proves that he faced it, and solved it.

His solution, through the discovery of the parabolic or elliptic mirrors, which eliminate the caustic, and reestablish a *focal point*, is geometrically equivalent, in avoiding of projective distortion between a curved surface and a plane, to using what is called "Gaussian" curvature, that is, the elliptic type. (**Figure 9.**)

But, projectively, Leonardo's solutions, through the compass of proportion, leads, if elaborated, to Desargues' theorem, and, more interestingly, to the establishing of proof of the projective invariance of the Golden Section.

As said, such *caustics* are second-order Beltrami surfaces; they are key. Briefly, they were then studied geometrically by Kepler, [Christiaan] Huyghens, but especially by [Gaspard] Monge. (**Figure 10.**)

A step further, and the same method, at least visually, leads to the graphic use of the *characteristic lines* by Riemann to describe the shock-wave [*On The Propagation of . . .*, 1859].

As we introduced this material here, the foregoing quotation, and accompanying figures supplied by de Paoli, were one of numerous responses to an earlier research memorandum. The issuance of that memorandum has a pre-history, which is relevant to the purpose of citing de Paoli's remarks and ilustrations in connection with the quadruply-connected geometry of the classical musical domain.

For more than two decades, this writer had been persuaded that the physical space-time curvature of sub-atomic microspace must be necessarily represented as a Riemannian space of harmonically ordered

Caustics

The light shining through a wine glass filled with liquid produces a caustic. The inset shows only the caustic, which is the envelope of rays emanating from a point, which are refracted or reflected by a curved surface.

Philip Ulanowsky

curvature. This view had been reworked into an hypothesis at the beginning of the 1970s. At that time, the practical function assigned to that hypothesis, was the mapping of the characteristic functions of development of the biosphere, on the working assumption derived from the hypothesis, that the primary location of the *negentropy* characteristic of both living processes and their interaction with inorganic processes, is located in the sub-atomic domain of microphysics, and that the physical geometry of that domain is itself representable as *negentropic* in Riemannian geometric terms of reference.

This writer had "shopped" the hypothesis into a number of the scientific seminars in which he participated. In 1985 and 1986, that hypothesis was taken up, and a crucial-experimental proof of it supplied. The evidence is now conclusive, that hypothesis is the correct one. On the basis of the submission and discussion of that proof, a number of new projects were set into motion, including a fresh approach to the determination of the Periodic Table of elements and isotopes.

Several of those lines of work, but the investigation of the Periodic Table's ordering of the protons and neutrons of the nucleus most emphatically, posed the importance of defining in a Riemannian way the *strong* nuclear forces. It became clear to this writer, that the referenced inadequacies in elaboration of the Riemann Surface Function were put at the center of the crucial-experimental work needed to address the proposed nuclear ordering.

For several reasons, Beltrami's treatment of negative curvature appeared to be a profitable line of approach. Some useful work by a young Italian researcher, completed a few weeks ago, prompted me to set this line of approach into high gear. What was needed to that purpose, was to define a multi-faceted, but coherent approach to several lines of investigation. In such a case, this writer resorts to a tactic which one senior physicist has described as "provocative hypothesis." A provocative memorandum was written and circulated, intended to provoke as many fruitful, parallel but converging lines of reflection and inquiry into motion as possible.

That was one of two memoranda on this matter, to which researcher Dino de Paoli responded in the manner indicated above.

Some of the considerations involved in that research memorandum bear directly on the relevance of this to the principles of musical composition. Those considerations are identified next.

Perspective constructions

A) Simple linear perspective

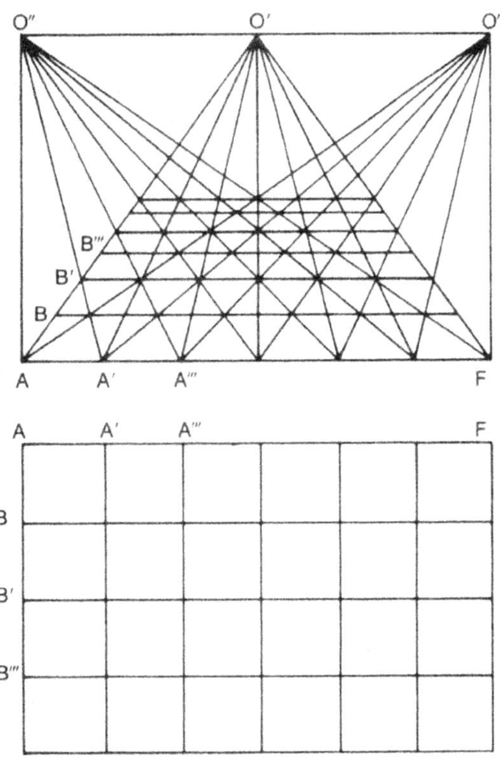

Implications of the Kantian Paradox

Whenever we are confronted with crucial evidence requiring us to overturn hallowed presumptions of prevailing scientific opinion, we must take two approaches simultaneously. We must direct our attention to relevant sorts of contemporary scientific work, but we must also examine both the conception we are overturning, and its proposed successor, from the standpoint of relevant features of the internal history of science.

We must examine the underlying assumptions of extant prevailing scientific opinion, in their character as assumedly axiomatic assumptions of method and ontology, and do this in a Socratic way. We must, simultaneously, examine the kindred roots of the kinds of notions of method and ontology we are putting forward as alternatives, variously explicitly and implicitly. We must also combine these two approaches to the relevant internal history of science, to trace the history of interaction between the tendencies toward, and conflicts among the contrasting views under consideration.

Since, in all such cases, we are addressing directly "axiomatic" qualities of conception of method and ontology, our attention is focussed almost entirely on that which is profound and simple, and to the crucial experimental evidence which always corresponds to the most profound, and hence simplest matters.

B) A simple reflection between linear perspective and a curved surface produces caustic points Instead of focal points.

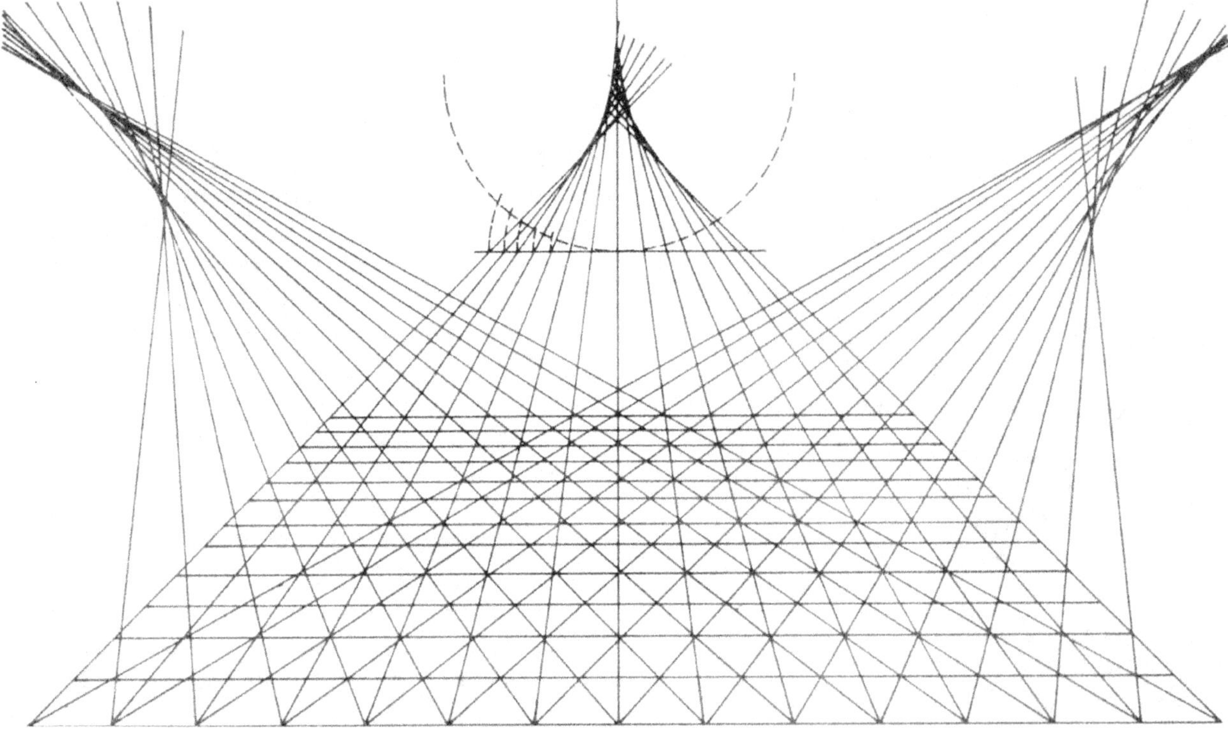

One of Leonardo da Vinci's Drawings of a Caustic

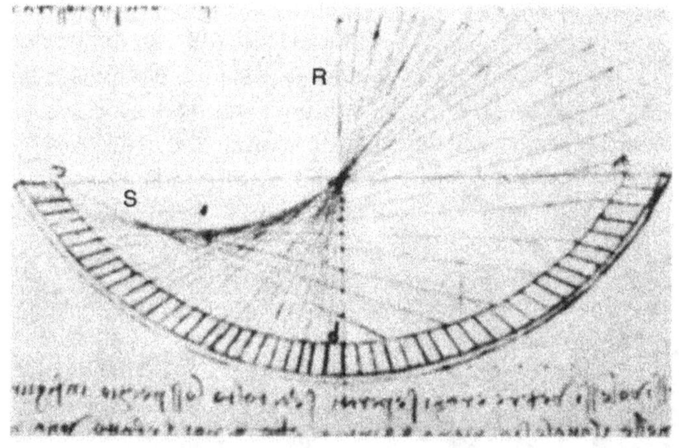

RS represents the caustic.

It is the case, that all of the fundamental laws of physics, and crucial evidence pertaining to fundamental laws, are always properly to be examined in terms analogous to the approach of Kepler. For reasons of the physics of non-euclidean geometries, fundamental physical laws are always rooted in congruence with a definite curvature of physical space-time. Indeed, any statement respecting the curvature of physical space-time, and any statement respecting elementary notions of universal physical laws are, respectively, but two ways of saying the same thing, as the instance of the *fine-structure constant* merely illustrates the point in an implicitly conspicuous way.

Contrary to the popularized delusions associated with a formal euclidean, deductive geometry, such as a Cartesian form of Newtonian or formal-statistical discrete manifold, all physical space-time is curved in effect. This curvature reflects a self-bounded character of physical space-time as a whole. This has two practical implications which must be drawn out here.

First, as Kepler's astrophysics illustrates this, the fundamental laws of motion in physics are not determined by the interaction, as "at a distance," between two bodies in empty space and empty time. The fundamental laws of motion exist independently of any bodies affected by them, and independent of any ideas commonly associated with a Cartesian or Neo-Cartesian sort of discrete manifold. Those laws exist everywhere in the universe, at all times, in a manner independent of any consideration associated with ideas analogous to a constant speed of light.

FIGURE 10

The Monge Envelope

A)

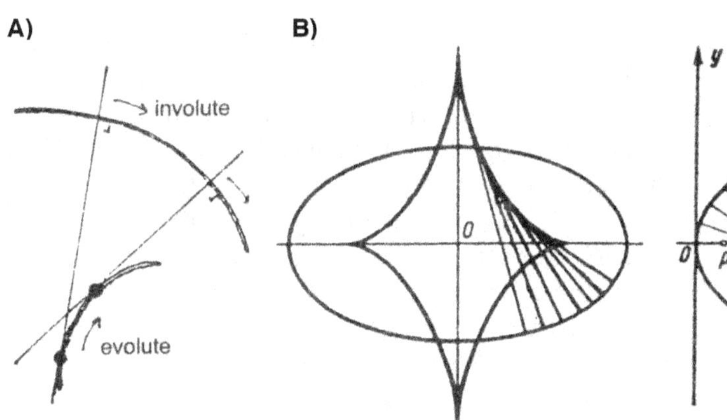

B)

C)

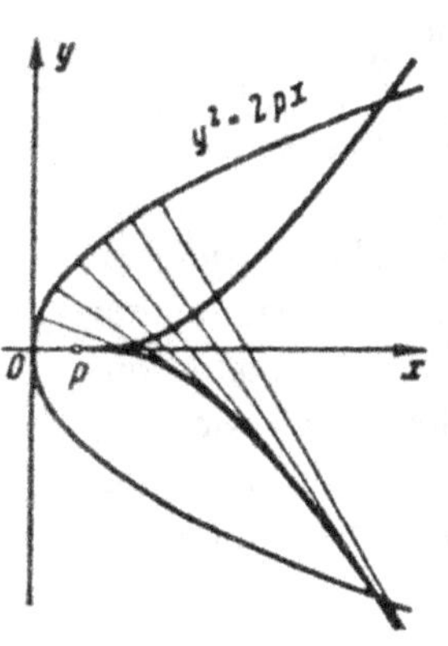

The "envelope" is a generic concept developed by Gaspard Monge for a curve enclosing other curves, or surfaces, touching all of them. The evolute is one of many possible such envelopes. The normals to a curve of non-constant curvature do not converge on a point, but rather form a new curve, or "evolute." Every curve has one, and only one, such reciprocal curve, respectively called the involute and evolute. The left hand diagram (a) shows the relationship of involute and evolute; the right-hand diagrams (b) show the involutes of the ellipse and parabola.

(c) Model built by Beltrami showing a Monge envelope in three dimensions. The very obvious curve of the sides of the figure does not physically exist, but is formed as the result of the series of straight strings.

In effect, every two-body problem is a three-body problem, in the sense that it is the interaction of each of two discrete bodies with the curvature of space-time, which determines their apparent motion with respect to one another.

Since Gauss, we have understood more clearly than before, that the adducing of the most elementary laws of physics depends upon discovering means by which we, with the limitations of our perceptual apparatus, might map the curvature of the physical space-time in which we exist. Implicitly, since the work of Nicolaus of Cusa, and the continuation of Cusa's work by Leonardo da Vinci and his associates, we have understood that there are three special domains of expe-

Immanuel Kant (1724-1804) claimed that creative processes for valid fundamental scientific discoveries are beyond all human understanding . LaRouche proved him wrong .

rience in which this mapping must be conducted. These three domains represent, geometrically, the extremes corresponding to the self-bounding of physical space-time as a whole. These three are, the extreme scale of astrophysics, the extreme scale of microphysics, such as sub-atomic microphysics, and the characteristics of all living processes which characterize the difference between living and non-living processes on the ordinary scale of perceptual experience.

No proposed law of the universe can be considered a law unless, and until it has been demonstrated to be characteristic commonly of all three boundary conditions: astrophysics, microphysics, and optical biophysics.

Whenever we examine the internal history of science respecting elementary issues of method and ontology, our retrospective view must be concentrated upon topics which either were, or ought to have been premised simultaneously on evidence bearing upon astrophysics, micrcophysics, and optical biophysics as domains in which crucial evidence is sought. On this account, the figures Nicolaus of Cusa, Leonardo da Vinci, and Kepler, are paradigmatic for strict usage of the term "scientist."

My own discoveries, bearing upon fundamental principles of economic science, have rendered intelligible a fourth boundary condition, the characteristic curvature

of those kinds of mental processes associated with generation of a valid fundamental discovery in science, processes otherwise exhibited in the instance a student, for example, effectively replicates, in his or her onw mind, the processes by which a valid fundamental discovery was originally constructed.

So, on the latter account, true education never bases itself upon a student's drill and grill in the mastery of isolated "facts." Rather, true education, as in the footsteps of Groote's Brothers of the Common Life, or the Humboldt reforms, devotes the greatest portion of the teacher's and student's attention to the student's reliving the mental experience of generating a past discovery. Defective education may produce students matriculating with high marks, but they are for the most part merely victims of a process not very much dissimilar from the programming of a moronic digital computer, to elevate it to the status of an "idiot savant."

So, today, we have graduates, even many with terminal degrees, graduating with highest marks, who are incurably bunglers whenever the assigned task requires real thinking. Such is the included effect, of the drift in the direction implied by "programmed learning."

My most important discoveries, in every field to which I have contributed, are based upon my successful refutation of the famous Kantian Paradox reasserted in Immanual Kant's *Critique of Judgment*. Kant asserted two things of relevance here.

First, he insisted that although creative processes responsible for valid fundamental scientific discoveries exist, these processes themselves are beyond all possible human understanding. That I proved to be false, and from that proof developed an approach to intelligible representation of those creative processes, and hence the implicit measurement of technological progress as such.

Second, on the basis of the first assumption, Kant argued that there were no intelligible criteria of truth or beauty in aesthetics. The toleration which has been gained so generally by all modern irrationalism in matters of art, has depended upon German and other acceptance of this thesis on aesthetics advanced by Kant and Carl Savigny later.

On condition that we show, that classical fine art depends upon the generating function of the same individual creative mental processes otherwise responsible for the generation and assimilation of valid fundamental scientific discoveries, and only on condition of that proof, are we able to supply valid general statements about "human nature."

It happens to be the case, that the ordering of the creative mental processes is characteristically *negentropic*, not in the way absurd, popularized "information theory" employs Ludwig Boltzmann's H-theorem, but in the way in which Leonardo's and Kepler's definition of the harmonic ordering of living processes is apprehended from the standpoint of the Gauss-Riemann constructive-geometric mapping of the complex domain.

In effect, the function of creative-mental processes to generate conscious, willful states of the human mind, as no animal species-member can do, and the further possibility of rendering these creative processes themselves conscious, by means of rendering them intelligible, represents man as a living process in whom the characteristic *negentropy* of living processes generally has become willful consciousness. In man, life is enabled to act upon itself by "free will," and upon the universe as a whole, too.

Since all formal knowledge of science and other matters is only relative, subject to future scientific revolutions, the question is posed implicitly to us: "How can we pretend to know anything?" The answer is, in terms of those kinds of thought we associate with simple irrationalism, or even with methods of deductive formalism, we know nothing with certainty, and are usually in more or less grave degree of error in our opinions. How, then, can be ascribe the authority of even relative certainty to science?

What we can demonstrate, is the increased per-capita power of mankind over nature as a whole through those processes subsumed by the term "technological progress." What we can show, in this way, is that "technological progress" to such effect is *truth*. This fact locates true knowledge uniquely in the relevant functioning of the creative mental processes, by means of which fundamental scientific progress is generated and assimilated. Formal, deductive statements are relatively true, only to the extent they borrow a shadowy authority from the functioning, not of formal-deductive processes, but of creative processes.

All human scientific, and artistic knowledge is so premised as relatively true knowledge. Thus, everything we might presume to know respecting the curvature of physical space-time depends ultimately upon this scrutiny of the mental processes by which knowledge is developed. Thus, self-consciousness of an implicitly intelligible representation of the individual's creative-mental processes, is a bounding condition, and implied test, to which all scientific opinion must be subjected. Hence, this, added to crucial features of astrophysics, microphysics, and optical biophysics, is the fourth bounding condition of all human knowledge respecting the elementary laws of the universe.

For reasons so implied, this view is the only vantage-point from which the essence of classical musical composition can be adduced.

Now, to the Point

This brings us to the juncture, at which the importance of Beltrami's work is shown, both in a general way, and then its bearing upon the principles of classical musical composition. Earlier, we have indicated that we can not be misled into treating the points of a Riemannian point-set as if they were "points" in the same sense euclidean deductive geometry defines points axiomatically. In music, the introduction of a *relative* harmonic or metrical dissonance occurs as the generation of a point in a Riemann Surface; hence, the general case and the musical case are conjoined.

For those readers unfamiliar with the author's proof, it is essential that we supply a summary of the most relevant features here.

To the degree mathematical-physics formalism adopts the standard of consistency associated with deductive method, the entirety of such a physics forms what is termed a theorem-lattice of the form analogous to a euclidean geometry premised upon an underlying set of arbitrary (i.e., unproven) assumptions classed as a set of axioms and postulates. In such a theorem-lattice, there exists no single consistent theorem which states anything which is not already implicitly asserted by the corresponding set of axioms and postulates. This connection is freuently referenced as "the hereditary principle."

Therefore, in the instance a crucial experiment demonstrates any consistent theorem of such a theorem-lattice to be false, this suffices, by virtue of the "hereditary principle," to prove that the underlying set of axioms and postulates contains something false. It therefore also demonstrates that the entire theorem-lattice of mathematical physics is permeated by a corresponding,

Mr. and Mrs. Lyndon LaRouche (at concert, lower right) have actively sponsored a musical renaissance. Other photos, clockwise from upper left: Baritone Piero Cappuccilli shows the difference in a Verdi aria sung at the scientific pitch of A = 432 and the modern, higher tuning, at a 1988 conference held by Helga Zepp-LaRouche's Schiller Institute in Milan; French 'cellist Eliane Magnan has recorded all the Bach solo suites at Mr. LaRouche's encouragement; violinist Norbert Brainin (former first violinist, Amadeus Quartet) and pianist Günter Ludwig at a Washington, D.C. benefit for Lyndon LaRouche's legal defense in December 1988.

"hereditary" axiomatic falsehood.

Let a theorem-lattice so discredited "hereditarily" be designated for referance as Lattice A. Any alteration of the set of axioms and postulates effected to correct the errors shown to exist in one theorem, as shown by a crucial experiment, defines therefore a second theorem-lattice, "hereditarily" consistent with the reformed, new set of axioms and postulates, the which we may designate for reference as Lattice B.

It may be the case, and often is, that it is suggested that several alternate modifications of Lattice A's existing set of axioms and postulates, might appear to satisfy the requirement of altering the crucial theorem in such a way as to appear to agree with the crucial experimental findings. Thus, we would have, in such a case, an implicit series of mutually-exclusive choices of theorem-lattices, B, C, D, and so on.

The question, which of these alternate lattices is the proper choice, is accomplished by treating every theorem in each such hypothetical lattice as if were implicitly a new crucial experiment. We require a new lattice which is not only consistent, but in which each derived theorem is in agreement with the relevant crucial experiments implicitly defined by that theorem. The completion of such a process, set into motion by a single crucial experimental disproof of one theorem of an existing mathematical-physics theorem-lattice, is the formal meaning of the term "scientific revolution."

Let us presume that the result of such a scientific revolution is Lattice B. Let us examine the result under two conditions: firstly, as a general condition, for all such cases; and, secondly, under a very specific, idealized condition.

In the general condition, by virtue of the "hereditary principle," no theorem of Lattice B is consistent with any theorem of Lattice A, and vice versa. Thus, there exists such a "logical gap," an ubridgable gulf, in fact, separating any possible theorem of Lattice B from any possible theorem of Lattice A. In formal, deductive mathematics, the name for such a "logical gap," is a *mathematical discontinuity*. In physics, the name for such a phenomenon, is a *physical singularity*. The notion of a "topological singularity," as referenced by de Paoli in his cited remarks, has the same significance.

In the ideal case, let us assume that the crucial experiment appears to require only the smallest possible degree of change in the underlying set of axioms and postulates. A change in the parallel postulate of euclidean geometry, as already implicit in Desargues' theorem, is an example of such an ideal case. Examine the logical gap, mathematical discontinuity, or singularity, generated between euclidean Lattice A and neo-euclidean Lattice B, by "hereditary" implication.

Since the "logical gap" so defined between the two respective theoreom-lattices is of the smallest degree possible, there exists no alternate theorem-lattice, alternate with respect to either Lattice A or Lattice B, which could make the resulting gap between the two lattices deductively intelligible.

That preliminary conclusion, reached by that route, subsumes what Kant mistook for a conclusive proof that the creative processes are not susceptible of intelligible representation for the human understanding.

It should be clear, without more explanation than merely mentioning that fact, that Kant's argument depends upon the presumption, like Descartes' and Newton's identical error before him, that his notion of a neo-Aristotelean deductive method is the purest form of human reason.

There is no innocence in Kant's assertion of this. The entirety of Kant's work, both before and after his distancing himself from Hume's "philosophically indifferent" turn to a radical form of empiricism, is devoted to the single purpose of seeking to extinguish even the memory of the work of Gottfried Leibniz from German thought. The central issue in this undertaking of Kant's, is the fact that all of Leibniz's work in science and statecraft depends upon a view of the implicit intelligibility of the creative process, to which Leibniz refers in such locations as his *Monadology*.

This issue brings us to a deeper problem of method and ontology than that explicitly represented by the problematics of deductive theorem-lattices. If crucial experimental evidence demonstrates the kind of discontinuity shown as a logical gap between two deductive theorem-lattices, to correspond functionally to the existence of a physical state, then, in that case, the crucial experiment suffices to demonstrate that all deductive method is premised upon pervasive methodological and ontological absurdity.

In that case, rather than correcting the set of axioms and postulates of Lattice A, we throw all of them out,

and deductive method and correlated ontological assumptions with them.

At this juncture, it is important to stress, for those readers unfamiliar with this distinction, that our remarks above referenced a change in the parallel postulate as generating not a "non-euclidean geometry," but rather a "neo-euclidean" one. This distinction bears in a crucial manner and degree upon the popularized error of representing a change in the parallel postulate as generating a "non-euclidean geometry," when this merely produces a "neo-euclidean" one. This is key to the pervasive nonsense to this effect, so widely advertised in efforts to represent Special and General Relativity; it is key to the formal reasons why the learned disputes upon the subject, whether Riemann curvature of physical space-time must incorporate the negative curvature of Beltrami, are such useless muddles.

By a "non-euclidean geometry," we signify a purely constructive geometry, which prohibits any set of deductive axioms and postulates, and prohibits any employment of the deductive method in the elaboration of the theorems of geometry, or of mathematical physics in general. The modern discoverer of "non-euclidean geometry" was Nicolaus of Cusa.

Narrowly, as he reports this fact in some among his sermons, Cusa discovered what modern textbooks identity as the *isoperimetric theorem* of topology, as a solution to the problem which Archimedes had treated in the latter's theorems addressing the subject of attempts to square the circle. In his *De Docta Ignorantia*, Cusa situates the results of that proof in a general form of solution for what is usually known as the Parmenides Paradox.

In a more limited respect, as this bears upon the matters immediately under consideration here, is the following.

The only consideration from which a non-euclidean geometry begins, is that the intelligibility of developments in this universe must be constructed by reference to nothing but the relative maximal result effected by the relative minimal action. This is the root of the famous central principle of physical science, as first rigorously defined by Leibniz: the universality of a principle of physical least action. This is Cusa's "Maximum Minimum" principle.

In the simplest case, this yields the isoperimetric theorem. What is the minimal perimeter encompassing the relatively largest area or volume? This proof defines the circle or sphere in a socratic way, to such effect that the proof is independent of any consideration employed in demonstrating it. The method of this proof is the nature of what Leibniz termed *analysis situs*, later termed *topology*. (There are different, defective guises of taught topology, but we may ignore them here.)

From this beginning, a *constructive* or *synthetic* geometry, otherwise the strict definition of a *non-euclidean geometry*, is elaborated. This is the basis for construction of Riemannian and Beltramian geometry, and thus the key referent for the propositions considered here. The paramount considerations here, are three:

1) That circular action is the root-notion from which the notion of physical least action is derived;

2) That circular action is the only standard of measure in physics;

3) That, to construct a geometry, we can not begin with less than doubly-connected circular action, and preferably triply-connected.

By "doubly-connected circular action," we signify that every circular action is acted upon, in every smallest imaginable interval, by a second circular action, upon which it acts, similarly, in turn. In "triply-connected circular action," a third circular action acts similarly upon, and is acted similarly upon, each of the two of doubly-connected circular action.

Such *multiply-connected circular action* suffices to generate points and so-called straight lines. Hence, at this instant, points cease to have any self-evident existence, since we have shown that they have a fully intelligible existence, as generated by construction. The same applies to the generation of so-called straight lines.

From this beginning, the entire scope of the theorems of plane and solid euclidean geometry is generated, solely by construction, never considering anything not generated by nothing more than *multiply-connected circular action. Hence, all sets of deductive axioms and postulates are outlawed from geometry, and mathematics generally, and the deductive method, too.* That is a *non-euclidean geometry.*

Gottfried Wilhelm Leibniz (1646-1716), like Leonardo da Vinci and Kepler before him, premised his physics upon a non-euclidean geometry of the type described here.

The physics of Leonardo da Vinci and Kepler is premised upon such a non-euclidean geometry, as is the physics of Leibniz after them.

Without nullifying anything in such a multiply-connected circular-action geometry, Gauss, Dirichlet, Riemann et al. produced a superseding form of *synthetic geometry*, upon which the work of Beltrami is also premised. In this higher *synthetic geometry*, we express circular action in the conic form of self-similar-spiral action: denoting, that in our universe, physical least action is expressed by a constant, self-similar increase, or decrease of the magnitude subtended by circular action.

In a strict application of multiply-connected circular action to physics, the extension of circular action in time is represented by a cylinder. Thus, we are obliged to replace the Cartesian, linear coordinates to which misinformed students are habituated by cylindric coordinates, with the understanding that each of the coordinates is part of a function of multiply-connected action. This carries us, in electromagnetism, for example, as far as Fourier Analysis.

Gauss carries us further. In place of cylindric coordinates, we have double-conical coordinates, expressing such included "elementary" functions as electrical potential, magnetic potential, and frequency, each and all multiply-connected. The multiple-connection of such conical (self-similar-spiral) coordinates is the generation of hyperbolic functions, as is the case in definition of *technology* in the science of physical economy.

The formal mathematical discontinuities generated by such hyperbolic functions might be termed "true singularities," to distinguish their existence and physical significance from the simple singularities (point, line, solids, hyper-solids) of multiply-connected circular action. This organization of physical space-time is the minimal condition for representing adequately the universe in which we exist.

These singularities are everywhere dense, to such effect that their density is harmonically ordered in the manner Kepler ascribes harmonic functions to a physical space-time whose self-bounding curvature is congruent with the harmonic orderings associated with the Golden Section. Indeed, the Golden Section is nothing other than the metrical characteristic of all projections of self-similar-spiral action upon a plane or onto a solid.

The generation of these singularities, and how space must be organized topologically to the effect that the continuity of action in physical space-time persists despite such singularities, is the subject of the successive work of Dirichlet, Riemann, and Weierstrass. This defines the mathematics of generalized non-linear functions.

This leads to the strongest of the theorems of Georg Cantor's elaboration of transfinite functions. The density of singularities within any interval of arbitrarily chosen smallness, of continuing non-linear action, is implicitly enumerable. A more adequate expression of that theorem conforms to a general theorem for relativistic physics.

The density of discontinuities per interval of action, as this occurs in the triply-connected conical coordinate system introduced as illustration, is the proper meaning of a measure of *physical potential*. Thus, in these terms of reference, we can construct *potential functions*, so defined, represented as surfaces in that triply-connected phase-space. These surfaces are surfaces of equal potential.

Singularities appear in a Riemann Surface as points, or topological singularities, as Dino de Paoli references this. The existence of those points, as topological singularities, poses a pair of interrelated problems. The first is more immediate, from the standpoint of what we have just reviewed; the second takes us directly to the matter of negative curvature.

"Points do not exist." Hence, a singularity in a Riemann Surface represents something other than a point as such. In part, this is already clear from the Riemann Surface Function itself. These points were generated by the kinds of hyperbolic functions associated with multiply-connected self-similar-spiral action, and are not to be apprehended as self-evidently existing points in any sense.

Our problem is, that in that form, we have left them represented as if they were points. We must recognize them as related to what de Paoli references as *caustics*.

To make short of it, once we treat these properly, as regions of negative curvature of physical space-time, the continued generation of the Riemann Surface Function to a higher order of topological connectivity, must follow.

This renders the unique ordering of the combinations of protons and neutrons, in the Periodic Table's array of elements and isotopes, most interesting, and also renders the so-called "neutrino problem" of nuclear-fission reactions most interesting. The necessity of the harmonically-ordered Archimedian-solid geometries, which coincide with that ordering of nuclei in the Periodic Table, if otherwise crucially demonstrated experimentally, shows, as de Paoli points toward this, that the apparent strong nuclear forces we must consider fall into place with the indicated role of Beltrami negative curvature as the characteristic of singularities in a Riemann Surface Function.

We are implicitly faced with an analogous state of affairs in the resolution of canonically lawful singularities generated by a quadruply-connected compositional process of classical polyphony.

Beethoven may not have been a specialist in the mathematical physics of the Gauss-Riemann domain, but he has, in a meaningful sense, mastered such principles in effect.

Music & Physics

We indicated above, that the fundamental progress of physical science requires us to move upward and backward historically at the same time. Backward, to search out those features of the internal history of science which account for the development of the ideas we must discard, and those to replace what we discard. In the search of the internal history of science, we must emphasize the study of the processes of the human mind, where ideas are generated, as much as the bounds of astrophysics, microphysics, and biophysics.

On this account, every advance in physics and related knowledge, must impel us to reexamine the creative processes' role in the creative features of classical fine art; at the same time we occupy our attention with the most profound and simplest of the crucial facts of physics qua physics.

This is much more than a formal requirement. If we compartmentalize ourselves to such effect, that one function of our mind, acting in one connection, is not efficiently aware of what the same function does in a different connection, we are to that degree schizophrenic, and everything we do partakes of a corresponding degree of schizophrenia.

The fallacy I attack is a widespread one, especially since the influence of Kant and Savigny fostered the idea of an hermetic separation of the methods and ontology of physical science from those of art and social practice generally. To save this civilization, we must end this false, schizophrenic dichotomy, and put the whole human being back together again, as if nothing different should ever have occurred.